BERNARD KOPS

Dreams of
Anne Frank

a play for young people

METHUEN D

Published by Methuen Drama

1 3 5 7 9 10 8 6 4 2

Production photographs used are by Roger Howard. All other photos are from the
Anne Frank Stichting.
Dreams of Anne Frank first published in the United Kingdom by Samuel French
This Methuen Student Edition first published 1997 by
Methuen Drama,
Random House, 20 Vauxhall Bridge Road, London SW1V 2SA

Random House Australia (Pty) Limited
20 Alfred Street, Milsons Point, Sydney,
New South Wales 2061, Australia

Random House New Zealand Limited
18 Poland Road, Glenfield
Auckland 10, New Zealand

Random House South Africa (Pty) Limited
Endulini, 5A Jubilee Road, Parktown 2193, South Africa

Random House UK Limited Reg. No. 954009

A CIP catalogue record for this book is available from the British Library

Papers used by Random House UK Limited are natural,
recyclable products made from wood grown in sustainable forests.
The manufacturing processes conform to the environmental
regulations of the country of origin

ISBN 0 413 71250 8

Typeset in 10pt/11pt Times by Wilmaset Ltd, Birkenhead, Wirral
Printed and bound in Great Britain by Cox & Wyman Ltd, Reading, Berkshire

Contents

I dedicate this book to Erica, my wife, and to my children and grandchildren

Acknowledgements and thanks to the Polka Theatre, London; Classworks of Cambridge; and to the Anne Frank Foundation, Amsterdam

Introduction

A few years ago, the Polka Theatre for young people carried out a survey to find out which subjects young people most wanted to see dramatized and produced on the stage. Two themes emerged that stood out amongst all others: the stories of two girls whose lives epitomized the highest expression of the human spirit. They were Anne Frank and Helen Keller. But what was the connection? Why were these two chosen above all others?

There is a certain symmetry and logic to these choices. Both themes are related, connected. Helen Keller was born blind and deaf, and from her birth she was shut away and isolated within the confines of her own dark world. Yet instead of languishing in despair she somehow managed to overcome her confinement and make contact with the outside world. Her example, her courageous journey from isolation brought hope to so many others long beyond her lifetime.

Anne Frank was also removed and cut off from a normal life. She too was isolated, shut away from the world and forced to live within the narrow confines of her hiding place, in an attic in Amsterdam. It is not surprising that young people identify with these two isolated girls. Many young people feel trapped and locked within themselves, are trying to grow up and make sense out of the senseless happenings going on in the world of adults around them.

But why was I chosen to dramatize Anne Frank? And why did I readily decide to accept that challenge?

In 1904 my father left his Jewish community in Amsterdam in order to try to make a living in London. He settled in the East End and married my mother whose parents were also poor Jews who hoped to find a better life in London. But poverty followed them. My parents had eight children and struggled to earn a living. The poverty persisted until the outbreak of the Second World War. I was thirteen years old at the time; roughly the same age as Anne Frank. But whereas I was allowed the luxury and joy of growing up and marrying and having a career and a family, children and grandchildren, Anne remains forever locked in time; an eternal adolescent.

As a child, I often used to wonder about my relatives back in Holland and sometimes we would get news of them. I dreamed of going there and was proud of my Dutch heritage. Just before the war broke out, a message arrived from Amsterdam. It begged us all to return to Holland. They were certain that Holland would remain neutral. We were assured that we would be safer there and would escape the horrors of the inevitable approaching war. But our poverty in London was intense and we used to go to the soup kitchen every evening, just to survive. My father, however, was now fired with the idea that we all had to return to Holland and safety. To make this possible, he needed just fifty pounds to pay the fare for the entire family. He tried to borrow the money. He tried to beg the money. He tried everywhere, everyone. But money was in short supply. He failed and I still remember him wailing. Thus we were thwarted from returning to Amsterdam, and thus we survived the death camps.

All our Dutch relatives went to their deaths. They evaporated into silence, forever. If my father had succeeded in borrowing the money, we all would have made the same journey as Anne; we would have been rounded up and sent to the transit camp at Westerbork and on from there to Auschwitz. Thus the vagaries of fate had intervened; thus I grew up as a committed witness for that lost community of the Jews of Amsterdam; my family and Anne Frank. I was able to easily empathize with Anne without any leap into the dark. Anne's eventual fate was my own family's fate. Therefore I knew I was the natural choice to write this play.

The work is a total imaginative creation. All the events and dialogue during the action are imagined and subjective. I created the characters, relationships and events purely from the depths of my mind. Memory has no absolute chronology. But how to find the real Anne? The flesh-and-blood Anne? The girl who lived and breathed beneath the legend? How to make a living legend become human? When Anne entered that attic in July 1942 she also entered history. But I was interested in *my* Anne. The Anne of flesh and blood. The subjective Anne. The Anne of dreams. This is why I was not interested in dramatizing the diary. I needed to take another route, to find that specific human being, to strip away the deification and bring her down to earth. In order to do this, I needed dream logic, movement and song. I needed to create subjective events and personalities. If Anne could not move around in the real world of Amsterdam she could move around in her mind. There, within her imagination, all is possible. Anne can travel to the Hollywood she dreamed about. She can go ice-skating; she can journey into the Black Forest in search of the gingerbread house; she can converse directly with Winston Churchill. She can get married. She can even assassinate Hitler and save her people. She can plead with the children of the world to bear witness to the madness of human beings. Another reason I qualified to do this play was my personal knowledge of Anne. In the fifties my first play, *The Hamlet of Stepney Green*, was translated into Dutch by Rosie Pool, a wonderful woman who was a close friend of Martin Luther King. Rosie was a famous Dutch–Jewish author and translator who joined the Dutch Resistance during the war. She had escaped from the Nazi transit camp at Westerbork, and her first task was to smuggle herself back into that camp and organize others. There she met and tutored Anne. Rosie talked to me endlessly about Anne, about her character and personality, her dreams and nightmares. All this information fed my imagination. She became a sort of close relative.

In the late fifties and sixties I visited Amsterdam constantly. There, I soaked myself in the background of the once-thriving Jewish community. I also visited the attic over and over again, to try to understand; to come to terms with Anne's fate and the fate of my own family. Their fate could so easily have been mine. It was in Anne's attic that the unquenchable spirit of the girl came across to me. Her background and spirit pervaded my dreams, invaded my life. *Dreams of Anne Frank* is not a dramatization of her diary. Rather, it is an original way of focusing upon the girl, to bring alive that unquenchable spirit and show how she managed to be creative in the darkest of times. To write the play, I went to the facts of her life for the spine of reality and to my imagination for the subjective matrix, the foundation of my drama.

Anne Frank and the Romanies

A phone call from Amsterdam. Would I like to go to Hungary
and help mount a production of my play *Dreams of Anne
Frank*? It is Barry van Driel from the Anne Frank Foundation.
They are about to tour their 'Anne Frank in the World'
exhibition over there and would like my play to accompany it.

He speaks fast; sounds neurotic; has this brilliant idea. The
actors should be Romany children and tour the play throughout
the country. 'People forget there were a quarter of a million
Roma murdered in the Holocaust. Their history is oral; never
properly recorded.' Normally I would never go chasing one of
my plays, but this sounds different; exciting.

When we meet I discover a driven man. Barry, a social
scientist, seems to be sitting on a volcano that will blow its top
any moment. He has the drive and energy of an American
businessman plus the liberal concern of a Dutch academic.

'Eastern Europe is a powder keg, Bernard. To hell with easy
options. Touring *Anne Frank* in the West? Piece of cake. Why
do it? To tell yet again about the Holocaust and that
remarkable young girl. So what? Who cares? But in Russia!
Armenia! Romania! Slovakia! Hungary! Nothing's been
learned. Racism! Nationalism! Prejudice! It's all simmering;
waiting to boil over.'

It begins to seem like his personal crusade.

'Listen Bernard, there's no money in this. There's just the
fact that you might be doing something really worthwhile; it's
a good cause. It's important.'

'At my time of life I should become a humanitarian?' I
reply. Next thing, Erica and I are on a plane to Hungary.

Budapest! An old song almost infiltrates; teases. 'I have lost
my heart in Budapest . . . in a city right under the moon . . .
where the gypsy bands have come to rest . . . and the
Danube . . .' We come across a vast, black, crumbling
building. We enter. It is not the headquarters of the Hungarian

Secret Police. It is The Café New York. The vast Art Deco/
Rococo interior hits between the eyes. The chandeliers. The
huge, ornate, ormolu-encrusted mirrors. Here journalists still sit
all day, writing their copy. Here poems are born, aborted. Here
middle-aged, over-painted ladies discuss discarded lovers. And
here come the tourists, necks craned at the Sistined ceiling.
The eternal pianist playing Listz. A throwback, lost in his
Austro-Hungarian glory. The somnambulist waiters float
around. They haven't yet heard the news, that Crown Prince
Ferdinand has been assassinated in Sarajevo.

The pianist, his eyes now swivelling, look across at me,
starts to play 'My Yiddisher Momma'. Funny! I didn't think I
looked particularly Jewish. The pianist nods, smiles, as if he's
read my reactions. His eyes tell me he knows it all, has seen it
all. His hands now conjure 'Gloomy Sunday'. It happens to be
Sunday. You can see how this song emerged out of those
Budapest streets. The beggars; the drawn faces of housewives
in supermarkets; the skinheads in the Metro entrance, selling
newspapers, Nazi insignia splashed on their T-shirts. Drunken
young men and old women, faces like railway junctions,
fighting an endless battle against poverty, pollution. Surviving
somehow. But inside Café New York, the coffee cups tinkle.

The pianist bows, takes a rest. A Romany violin quartet take
the floor. 'If I was rich man . . .' The American tourists laugh
and drink Tokaj. A crocodile of Germans arrive. The Roma
quickly switch to Viennese waltzes. It is all so beautifully
blatant. The Roma band roam the restaurant, dispensing their
romantic Unismaltz, hither and thither. Ah! The gypsy way of
life. Their quaint carefree lives under the stars. How romantic
the Romany raggle-taggle gypsies! But an old poem niggles.
'My mother said I never should play with the gypsies in the
wood.' Those sentiments are no longer politically correct back
home, but here. . . . ?

I hate being a tourist, loathe seeing the sights. So, here, I wander
the back streets, take in the cafés; the old ghetto. Travel crowded
trams, the underground. And I soon smell out the pervading
pollution of nationalism; see overt discrimination. Here, the Roma
are known as 'the blacks'. Unemployment for Hungarians stands
at twenty per cent; for the Roma sixty-five per cent. Here it's all in

the open. It's everywhere. The Roma are treated worse than second-class citizens.

I stand before one of the biggest synagogues in the world. Police stand guard. It's being totally renovated for the grand re-opening in September. It's costing millions. Tony Curtis is picking up the bill. Barbara Streisand is doing the launch.

I'm starving. And suddenly I realize I'm free from the nemesis of the BSE cloud that hovers over Great Britain. I indulge in a glorious bowl of goulash soup, and Barry smiles, unwraps his idea. 'Bernard, we are going to show the world what these Roma kids can do.'

The play is to be performed by the Romany children from the Mahatma Gandhi school in Pécs, in the south of the country. A state boarding-school; the only Roma secondary school in the whole of Hungary. Here the precious few have a chance to go on to university. Three hundred kids out of a Roma population of approximately half a million.

We travel to Pécs. The Gandhi kids are alert, cheeky, clever; just like the kids of any inner-city comprehensive in Britain. One difference; these are incredibly polite; want to hold your hand or arm. '*Nem problem!*'

But there is just one fly in the goulash. They have no concept of theatre; most have never even been to the theatre. They do not know what a play is. Barry reminds me that he never promised a rose garden.

'Barry! Here I am approaching the foothills of middle age. These kids don't know how to move, to project, to stand.' I realize it is up to me to impose some kind of shape. I conjure up remembered magical words of Martha Graham. 'Discipline is freedom.' Slightly incongruous, I think; and I am right. The interpreter translates. The kids smile back at me. And jive. I try to teach a teacher how to mount a play. I am getting too old for this sort of thing. If my hair hadn't already turned white, it would now. It is decided to hire a professional director. No sooner is the decision made than a swarm of directors descend. I am left to do the interviewing.

Mihaly is all smiles. He is breathing heavily, his clothes are threadbare; he is extremely thin. I feel sorry for him. Everyone here is desperate for cash.

'You've written a beautiful play. A great play.'

I ask him if he's seen it. Or even read it. 'No. Not actually.'

He sees from my frown that he's a no-goer so he wanders down to the Romany kids warming up on the stage, starts talking to them. Soon he is doing a workshop with them. I feel bad when I order him out of the gymnasium but he continues his chat. I ask Joseph, the play's translator, to translate. *'Nem problem.'* I press Joe further. 'He's actually telling them that you and your play are utter crap.' You have to laugh. We finally take on Marta Barta. She runs a children's theatre in Budapest. She seems as if she can cope. What can you do? You have to take chances.

Night. We sleep in the school. No loo paper. No locks on the doors. Mosquitoes are not prejudiced; they'll drink the blood of anyone. Romany. Jew. Dutchman. I read up the Roma history. They came from India ten centuries ago; the language derives from Sanskrit. Their poetry reminds me of Lorca. Their folklore is beautiful; 'Romanies once were birds who came to earth and forgot how to fly. We do not settle because one day we will become birds again.' 'The world is a ladder. Some go up and some go down.' Most Romanies certainly go down. But not these kids in this unique school. They are dedicated, determined, direct and beautiful.

We open in Szeged; a most beautiful town in the south. I like this place. Here people are relaxed, smile. And there they are, my Roma children, up on a real stage, doing my play. They are moved by the play; and therefore move us. It is Amsterdam, 1942. The Romany children are suddenly Jewish people in hiding; about to meet their fate. There is Romany Anne, getting married to Romany Peter, under the Chupah, the Jewish wedding canopy. And there they go, into the darkness of death. Anne's final plea to the world's children before she goes into the 'Night and Fog'. It is too much to bear. A quarter of a million Romanies died in that same Holocaust. The parallels of our two people's fate cut deep.

But what of the performances? The production? Let me say that in this instance the play was not as important as the playing. The text had been cut by half and the director had taken great liberties with its expressionistic style. The songs were gone. But nothing's perfect in this world and it is sheer miracle that it came to life at all.

'You are not disappointed?' The anxious director asked. 'You do understand?' Barry and I nodded approval. His smile was enough of a benediction. Four TV camera crews are in attendance. This is obviously a big deal. A first.

The Deputy Mayor of Szeged approaches. She hands me a silver medallion. 'Wonderful. I am amazed that Roma children could do this.' I want to spit. This is the way it goes in Hungary. Later, we all eat pizzas in the big square. Later still, we all go to a disco. The kids dance with joy, relieved it's all over. For the moment. They double up with laughter at our attempt at the Twist. They crowd around and clap. I'm getting homesick. 'I'm too long in the tooth for this sort of thing.'

'Never mind. Next year, Bratislava; Slovakia!' Barry's eyes light up with thoughts of another coming challenge.

'I hear it's even worse there. The nationalism; the prejudice,' I shout back.

'It's all worth while. All in a good cause.' Barry is also dancing, but he leans over to inform me that the play is soon to be performed in one of the kids' villages; and, would you believe it, the venue is to be in the small Catholic church. I'm stunned. My words at last will infiltrate their holy of holies. The story of Anne and her dreams will be re-enacted there, before their altar. My dead Jews will enter the hearts of those who set the whole terrible thing in motion.

So the Roma and the Jews finally win out. Who says there ain't no justice? I laugh. I can just see a furious Pope Pius XII spinning in his grave. Erica and I continue dancing.

A version of this article originally appeared in the *Guardian* newspaper.

Historical Background

Germany and the road to war

Germany was in total chaos after the First World War. The victors demanded huge sums of money to pay for the devastation caused by the war. In Germany, inflation soared and the currency became worthless. The economy stagnated, millions of people were out of work and small businessmen and small shopkeepers were ruined. People were literally starving. There was no welfare system to protect people, and bitterness grew.

The National Socialist Party offered an end to indecision and uncertainty. They were a fascist group and their ideology was based on lies and prejudice. They believed that their own race was superior to all others, and that men were intrinsically superior to women. They rejected democracy and believed that blind obedience to one leader was essential. They wanted their nation to consist only of people like themselves, so that anyone who was obviously different from them – from a different race, someone who was weak, ill, or had special needs – should be removed for the sake of racial purity. In addition, they wished to expand German territories, which would increase German wealth.

By 1933, the Nazis had gained 44 per cent of the votes, rising to 56 per cent including the support for the nationalist parties. The opposition parties never attempted to unite effectively at the polls, and by the time they realized how dangerous the Nazis were, they had been imprisoned or were on the way to the concentration camps.

Economics are not often easily understood. So when the Nazis identified the Jews as the enemies of Germany, responsible for leading Germany into the last disastrous war and for destroying the German economy, many people were all too ready to identify them as scapegoats. This, of course, was absurd, but the majority of the German people was happy with this 'simple' solution. Initially, the Nazis passed some very restrictive and humiliating laws restricting the freedom of Jewish people in Germany, and later in the countries invaded by Germany. These culminated in their imprisonment and murder in concentration camps. By the end of the war, the Nazis were responsible for the murder of over six million Jews, intellectuals, communists, Romanies, homosexuals and anyone else too different or too outspoken against the German government.

The Frank family – Frankfurt

Ancestors of Anne Frank had lived in Frankfurt since the seventeenth century. Otto Frank, Anne's father, was born on 12 May 1889, on Frankfurt's Westend (West side), a well-to-do neighbourhood. His father was a banker. Otto Frank attended high school, and briefly studied art at the University of Heidelberg.

Via a friend, he was offered and accepted a job from 1908 to 1909 at Macy's department store in New York. When his father died, Otto Frank returned to Germany and worked for a metal engineering company in Dusseldorf until 1914. During World War I, he and his two brothers served in the German Army, where Otto attained the rank of lieutenant. After the war he worked in his father's bank, but banks were not faring well at that time. While at the bank, he became acquainted with Edith Hollander, the daughter of a manufacturer. Born in 1900, she grew up in Aachen. Otto and Edith married in 1925 and settled in Frankfurt. They had two daughters, Margot, born in 1926, and Anne, whose full name was Annelies Marie, born on 12 June 1929.

The Frank family – Holland, 1933–1940

In 1933, after Hitler's seizure of power and the anti-Jewish boycott, Otto Frank left Frankfurt for Amsterdam. He started a branch of the German Opekta Co. there, and soon Edith, Margot and Anne joined him.

The Frank family moved into a house on Merwedeplein in the southern part of the city. Anne and Margot attended the Montessori School nearby. They had lots of friends, and photographs show the many excursions they took. The Franks became good friends with some other Jewish emigrants who settled in the same neighbourhood. The Opekta Co. was doing rather well.

However, this apparent carefree life was suddenly interrupted by the German invasion in May 1940.

May 1940: occupation of Holland

The German invasion began on 10 May 1940, and was a complete surprise. Holland expected to remain neutral as it had done during World War I.

The occupation was swift. In a few days all important areas were seized. The Prime Minister and his cabinet, as well as the Royal Family, fled to England. After fierce fighting near Arnhem and the bombing of Rotterdam, Holland was forced to surrender. As of 15 May 1940, the country was under German occupation.

The first measures

After the first shock and terror of the military actions, most Dutch were relieved that the Germans were behaving 'properly'. The majority of Dutch did not question the right of the Germans to impose their rules. Some measures taken by the Germans, like the blackouts, seemed reasonable: others seemed bearable, such as the introduction of the ID card.

Since Germany seemed invincible, it stood to reason one should adapt to the inevitable. The large majority of civil servants, teachers and judges – as well as the Jews among them – filled out the 'Declaration of Aryanism'. The socialist trade union got a National Socialist Bond director, but most trade union leaders wanted to stay to salvage as much of their organization as possible. Thousands of members dropped their union membership. A number of politicians established a new political organization – the Dutch Union – which was anti-

National Socialist but accepted the changed situation. In practice they did not oppose the German occupation. After a year, however, the union was also banned.

Labour service

Germany lacked trained labour, especially after millions of Germans were drafted for military service. During the occupation unemployed Dutchmen were forced to work in Germany. In May 1941 the number reached 165,000. In April 1942 a forced labour service was introduced for students and those who wanted to join the civil service. Many tried to avoid the service. In the last years of the occupation the Germans seized men and boys at random from the streets and sent them to Germany to work.

The first razzia (round-up)

That the Germans meant business in Holland became clear in February 1941. The WA, the paramilitary arm of the NSB, repeatedly entered the Jewish neighbourhood of Amsterdam, displaying aggressive and brutal behaviour.

Markets on Waterloo Square at Amstelveld were raided. The inhabitants of the Jewish neighbourhood organized groups to defend their property. Heavy fighting ensued. When a WA man died, the Germans retaliated. On 22 February the Jewish neighbourhood was sealed off and 400 Jewish men and boys were grabbed off the streets and from houses and coffee shops, beaten and taken away. No one knew where they had gone.

The February strike

To protest against this razzia, a general strike was organized immediately, primarily by the Communist Party. In and around Amsterdam, thousands joined in a two-day strike, making it the most influential act of resistance during the war. The Germans retaliated with force. German troops were sent in to restore order. Shots were fired. People were arrested. For fear of further reprisal, the strike ended on 27 February.

Endlosung ('the final solution')

When Germany marched through Eastern Europe, the army was followed by SS special units (*Einsatz Gruppen*) that started the mass execution of Jews. More than one million Jews were shot.

In 1941 the decision was made 'to make Europe clean of Jews'. During the Wannsee Conference in January 1942 plans were made to annihilate the eleven million European Jews. The plans became known as the *Endlosung*, the 'final solution of the Jewish question'.

Destruction and labour camps were built. A large number of the deported Jews – mostly the elderly, mothers and children – were gassed immediately upon arrival. The others had to work for a couple of months, until they died of exhaustion. In this way nearly six million Jews were killed. In addition to the Jews, countless others died in the concentration camps: political opponents, homosexuals, Jehovah's Witnesses, 'anti-social elements', Russian prisoners of war and at least 220,000 gypsies.

Deportation of the Jews

Most razzias and transportation activity to the camps occurred at night. In Amsterdam most Jews were first brought to the Jewish Theatre and then on to Westerbork. The majority stayed there several weeks, some more than a year.

In 1943 one transport followed another until the camp was full and life became unbearable. Westerbork, however, was not a final destination. Rather, it was a collection point to transport the Jews to the extermination camps.

Collaboration

The Dutch National Socialist organizations, of which the NSB was the largest, co-operated with the Germans. Even after the razzia in February they organized mass meetings to demonstrate their anti-Semitic and pro-German attitudes.

There was also collaboration based on the self-interests of

people who hoped to profit from the German occupation in Holland. This ranged from selling cakes to the German Army to building military installations.

Collaboration: SS volunteers

The Germans, using deep-rooted anti-communistic feelings, solicited volunteers for the war in Eastern Europe. No less than 30,000 Dutch men and boys signed up for the Waffen SS, and 17,000 were admitted, beginning in April 1941. Another 15,000 volunteered for military auxiliary organizations and police groups.

Resistance

Although most Dutchmen were anti-German or became that way once they were confronted with shortages and terror, they did not automatically choose to join the Resistance. Many factors immobilized them: fear, a fundamental rejection of civil disobedience, and religious principles based on the need to obey any government in power. But mostly, the (false) choices between fascism and communism immobilized the Dutch. For those who did resist, political and religious differences hampered the coordination of the Resistance, especially in the first year of the occupation. The first acts of resistance were mostly symbolic. In 1942 and 1943 a more efficient resistance movement developed.

The beginnings of the deportations: going into hiding, betrayal and resistance

Starting in January 1942, unemployed Jewish men were called upon to report for work in eastern Holland. Next, not only men, but entire families were summoned to go to Westerbork, a camp that served as a collection point. From there they were transported to what were called labour camps.

The Jewish Council was pressured to deliver the required numbers for transportation to Westerbork. When the quotas were not met, Jews were arrested at random. Thousands of Jews decided not to go and tried to hide.

The Frank family – going into hiding

During 1941 the number of anti-Jewish measures increased, and the Franks started preparing to go into hiding. Thanks to the co-operation of his staff (Mr Kraler, Mr Koophuis, Miep Gies and Elli Vossen), Otto Frank was able to secretly prepare a hiding place for his family and the van Daans (Mr van Daan worked with Otto Frank's company).

On 4 July 1942, Margot Frank received the notorious call to report to a 'labour camp'. The next day the Frank family moved into the 'Secret Annex'. One week later Mr and Mrs van Daan and their son Peter joined them, followed by Mr Dussel.

Tightening of the repression and resistance

In the spring of 1943 the German military lost ground. Allied advances in North Africa, the Soviet counterattack and the fall of Mussolini stimulated the Resistance. But simultaneously, repression for the remaining Dutchmen was increased.

In September 1944, of the non-Jewish population 250,000 were hiding; 12,500 were prisoners of war; 7000 were political prisoners; and 300,000 forced labourers. Aside from those groups, about 900,000 people were forced to leave their homes and move. The total population in Holland then was about nine million. Starting from the summer of 1944, many Resistance fighters were shot. Hundreds of others were executed in retaliation for acts of resistance.

The Frank family – the end

On 4 August 1944, the German police made a raid on the 'Secret Annex'. All the occupants were arrested and sent to concentration camps. They had been betrayed.

D-day and the liberation of southern Holland

In 1944 the Allied Forces gained momentum in Europe. The
Germans retreated from Eastern Europe. The liberation of
Western Europe began with D-Day. In one day, 6 June 1944,
156,000 Allied soldiers landed in northern France.

Following the successful invasion, rumours about the
liberation began. In Holland on 5 September 1944, known as
'Mad Tuesday', most people believed the liberation was near.
Southern Holland was, in reality, liberated.

Winter of hunger

The Dutch Railway halted service in September 1944 because
of a railway strike ordered by the Dutch Government in exile
in London. As a result, the Germans retaliated by forbidding
food to be brought to the cities. An enormous shortage
resulted, worsened by food confiscated by the Germans.

When coal and other fuel were not delivered to the cities,
the situation became critical. Everything that could be burned
was used for heat. Everything was eaten, even tulip bulbs.
Thousands of children were sent to the countryside to be fed.
About 22,000 people died of hunger. Tens of thousands were
seriously ill. Meanwhile, the Germans took anything of value
to Germany: bicycles, machines, factory equipment, street cars
and cattle, for example.

The starving ends as Holland is liberated

In April 1945 the English dropped food over starving Holland,
allowing many thousands to survive. The announcement was
made over British Radio.

A few weeks later the war was over. The remainder of
Holland was liberated by the Allied Forces. Festivities were
organized throughout the country. At the same time the Nazis
and their collaborators were arrested.

The publication of Anne Frank's diary

After the people in hiding had been taken away, the helpers returned to the Annex and took as much as possible before the Annex was cleared.

Miep had kept Anne's papers during that time. Upon his return to Amsterdam, Otto Frank realized he was the only survivor of his family. Miep Gies gave Anne's papers and writings to him. Friends persuaded Otto Frank to publish Anne's diary. *The Diary of Anne Frank* appeared in 1947 under the title *Het Achterhuis* ('The Annex').

To date, more than fifty different editions have appeared, and more than eighteen million copies have been sold. In 1953 Otto Frank married Elfriede Markovits, also a survivor of Auschwitz. They settled in Basel, Switzerland, where Otto Frank died in August 1980, at the age of ninety-one.

The house where Anne and the others lived is now a museum, operated by the Anne Frank Foundation, which was founded in 1957. Apart from the preservation of the Annex, the Foundation tries to stimulate the fight against anti-semitism, racism and fascism with information and educational projects.

Neo-Nazis and the denial of the Holocaust

Following the end of World War II in 1945, Nazism and fascism did not disappear. In a number of countries small groups soon emerged and their ideas and appearance bore a great similarity to the old movement. Moreover, countless people who supported the Nazi regime were allowed to live in complete freedom and re-establish themselves in society. A small number of organizations openly admit their sympathy for fascism in its old form, and they deny its crimes.

'The hoax of the twentieth century' is how Neo-Nazi groups label the mass murder of Jews by the Nazis. By denying the crimes of Nazi Germany, they try to rehabilitate National Socialism. Sometimes this takes the form of a so-called objective, historical discussion that in no way reminds us of uniformed Nazi groups and therefore is even more dangerous. To augment their following and to acquire a base of political support, these groups try to be accepted as honest, civil organizations.

Political and Military Events

7 March 1936	Germany occupies the demilitarized Rhineland.
12 March 1938	Austria's annexation.
29 September 1938	The Munich Treaty. France and Great Britain agree to the occupation of Sudetenland.
23 August 1939	Nonaggression pact between Germany and the Soviet Union; Poland divided between them.
1 September 1939	Germany invades Poland.
3 September 1939	France and Great Britain declare war on Germany.
9 April 1940	Germany invades Denmark and Norway.
10 May 1940	Germany invades Holland, Belgium, Luxembourg and France.
27 August 1940	Germany, Italy and Japan form a pact.
12 September 1940	Germany invades Romania.
6 April 1941	Germany invades Yugoslavia and Greece.
7 December 1941	Japan attacks Pearl Harbor.
8 December 1941	The United States declares war on Japan.
11 December 1941	Germany and Italy declare war on the United States.
7 November 1942	American and British troops land in North Africa.
2 February 1943	The German 6th Army capitulates at Stalingrad.
10 July 1943	Allied landing in Sicily.
4 June 1944	Liberation of Rome.
6 June 1944	Allied invasion in Normandy, France (D-Day).
22 June 1944	Russian advance on the Eastern Front.
20 July 1944	Lt. Col. von Stauffenberg perpetrates a bomb attack against Hitler. Attack fails.

11 September 1944	American soldiers reach the border of Germany.
4 February 1945	Conference in Yalta. The United States, Great Britain and the Soviet Union discuss the division of spheres of influence in Europe.
5 May 1945	Liberation of Holland.
8 May 1945	The German Army surrenders unconditionally.
6 August 1945	Atomic bombs on Hiroshima and Nagasaki force Japan to surrender.

Important dates in the lives of the Frank family

1926		Margot Frank, Anne's sister, is born in Frankfurt am Main in Germany.
1929	12 June	Anne Frank is born in Frankfurt am Main, Germany.
1933		Adolf Hitler becomes Chancellor of Germany.
		Boycott of Jewish businesses begins.
		All German Jewish Civil Servants are fired.
		Frank family leave Germany and go to Amsterdam.
		They move into a house in Merwedeplein in South Amsterdam.
1934		Anne goes to Kindergarten.
1940		Mr Frank starts a spice business at 263 Prinsengracht.
	May	German armies invade the Netherlands which surrender after 5 days, and the Occupation begins.
1941		Margot and Anne enter a Jewish Grammar School.
1942	12 June	Anne receives her diary as a birthday present and starts writing.
		Household effects are secretly carried over to the Annexe.
	July	Margot receives papers ordering her to register for mandatory work.
	6 July	The Franks move into the Annexe.
	13 July	The van Daan family moves into the Annexe.
1944	1 August	Anne's last diary entry.
	4 August	The inhabitants of the Annexe arrested by the German Military Police.
	8 August	All Annexe people to Westerbork transitcamp.
	3 Sept	All transported to Auschwitz Concentration Camp.
	6 Sept	Mr van Daan killed.
	26 Sept	Mrs van Daan transported to Bergen-Belsen Concentration Camp.

	Oct/Nov	Margot and Anne transported to Bergen-Belsen.
	Dec	Mr Dussell dies in Neuengamme Concentration Camp.
1945	Jan	Mrs Frank dies of starvation in Auschwitz. Mr Frank is liberated from Auschwitz by the Russian army and taken to a hospital. Peter van Daan is transported to Mauthausen.
	Feb	Mrs van Daan sent to Buchenwald, then in April to Theresienstadt, but dies by the 9th of May.
	March	Margot and then Anne contract typhoid and die within days of each other in Bergen-Belsen.
	May	Peter dies in Mauthausen. German Army surrender.
	June	Mr Frank returns to Amsterdam.
1947		The *Diary of Anne Frank* is published. It is first published in Dutch. French, English and German translations follow.
1960		The Secret Annexe is opened as a Museum.
1997		The 'definitive' edition of Anne's diary is published, with previous deletions restored.

About the Play

Why do a play about Anne Frank for young people?

Dreams of Anne Frank was specially commissioned by Polka Theatre to commemorate the fiftieth anniversary of Anne Frank going into hiding. August 4 1994, marked the fiftieth anniversary of the betrayal of the Frank family to the Gestapo and their subsequent deportation.

Bernard Kops has used Anne Frank's diary and record of her two years in hiding to investigate the imagination and dreams of a young adolescent girl who wanted so much to be a writer. The world is still full of prejudice and we must try to make young people aware of it so they can change it for the better. Anne Frank was a brave young person whose story and talent should be shared. Her diary is accessible to young people because it is written simply with little self pity and great humour.

I have received many thousands of letters. Above all it is younger people who wish over and over again to find out how such dreadful events could come about. Often, at the end, I write: 'I hope that Anne's book will influence your later life to work, as far as your circumstances allow, for peace and reconciliation!'

Otto Frank, Anne's father, 1979

My story is a story of very ordinary people during extraordinary times; times the like of which I hope with all my heart will never come again. It is for all of us ordinary people all over the world to see to it they do not.

Miep Gies, one of the Dutch helpers who kept Anne and the others alive.
From *Anne Frank Remembered*, 1987

To create a play about Anne Frank for young audiences is not easy. It cannot tell all the story, it can only go some way to opening young ears and eyes. The full horror they must assimilate at their own pace in response to the questions the play raises. In conclusion *Dreams of Anne Frank* is a play of substance which treats its young audience as intelligent and perceptive and talks to them on their own terms.

Vicky Ireland, Artistic Director, Polka Theatre

Anne Frank has to be more to us than a legend. She wanted to 'go on living' after her death and her story can pose essential questions to young audiences now about the issues of racism, nationalism, war, genocide, human rights and individual responsibility – would we have stood by and watched . . . or would we have put our lives in danger to help such a family as the Franks? Do we stand by now and watch things happening that we know to be wrong? The end of our play focuses very strongly on these subjects as contemporary questions. Otto Frank, Anne's father and sole survivor of the family, felt strongly that Anne's diary should be used in a way that would educate young people about these issues and open their eyes not only to the lessons of the past but also to the realities of the present. In 1992 4,140 racial incidents were reported in London and in recent weeks a judge in Newcastle has said that the number of racist attacks last year had risen by 300 per cent. It is easy to be complacent about racism if you think it doesn't affect you personally, but the responsibility is shared by everyone of us.

The importance of design in *Dreams of Anne Frank*

The design team have tried to create Anne's Dream World using the characters and objects which were around Anne before and during her time in the Annex. Everything is through her eyes. We have not tried to recreate the Annex. This play is about feelings, about growing up, about the loss of freedom and the loss of the natural elements which normally surround us (rain, snow, trees, flowers) and the wonderful world we can all create in our 'imagination'. The set and costumes will reflect this.

Fran Cooper, Designer

References in the Play

Auschwitz   Concentration camp in Poland where the Frank family were initially sent. Edith Frank died here of starvation two months after her daughters. Anne and Margot were transported on to Bergen-Belsen where they both died of typhus. Otto Frank, Anne's father, survived and was liberated from Auschwitz by Russian soldiers. Auschwitz was more than a concentration camp – it was a death camp of which there were six, all in Poland, specifically set up to complete the 'final solution' – total extermination of the Jews. These camps were: Auschwitz, Majdanek, Treblinka, Sobibor, Chelmno, Belzec. Among the sixteen concentration camps where hundreds of thousands died from disease, starvation, random brutality, human experimentation, etc were Plaszow, Buchenwald, Dachau, Ravensbruck, Theresienstadt, Bergen-Belsen, Mauthausen. It is important also to remember that other groups were persecuted by the Nazis – including Gypsies, communists, homosexuals and the mentally and physically handicapped.

The yellow star   All Jews were required by the Nazis to wear a yellow Star of David as a 'badge' to identify them.

Call up   The Franks had been preparing, with the help of their Dutch friends, to go into hiding for some time. Their decision to do so was escalated by the fact that Margot received notification to report to the police. She would probably then have been deported to a camp in Germany. This was a means by which Jews were rounded up and transported to concentration camps in Poland, Germany, Austria and Czechoslovakia.

***Mein Kampf*/Nuremberg Laws**   Hitler wrote *Mein Kampf* before he came to power and it was published in 1925. In it he expounded his philosophy based on the purity of the German master race and also expressed his virulent anti-semitic feelings. After he became Chancellor in 1933 sales of *Mein*

Kampf reached one million. By 1940 six million copies had
been sold and Hitler was a millionaire. The Nuremberg Laws
of 15 September 1935, signed by Hitler, set out the rules for
'the Protection of German Blood and German Honour'. Under
the first law, Citizens could only belong to a nation of German
or kindred blood. Under the second law, all Jews were defined
as being not of German blood.

Wannsee Conference   In the play, Edith Frank speaks to her
husband of the times they went boating on Lake Wannsee.
Wannsee, of course, does not have pleasant memories. It was
on 20 January 1942 in a villa on the shores of the lake that
Heydrich explained his aims as 'Plenipotentiary for the
Preparation of the Final Solution'. This 'final solution'
concerned eleven million Jews throughout Europe. Throughout
the forty four days prior to this conference more than 40,000
Jews and Gypsies had been murdered in experimental gassings
at Chelmno. The uprooting and total disappearance of whole
communities had been achieved and what had hitherto been
tentative, fragmentary and spasmodic was to become formal,
comprehensive and efficient. The 'solution' was the installation
of death camps in Poland.

Emigration   The Frank family left Germany in 1933, after the
election of Adolf Hitler, and emigrated to Holland. This
became more and more difficult for Jews as the years passed,
since so many countries were unwilling to accept Jewish
immigrants. In 1938 the U.S.A. convened the Evian
Conference. Australia announced: 'As we have no real racial
problem, we are not desirous of importing one.' The British
Empire had no territory suitable, New Zealand would not lift
restrictions, France had reached saturation point. Nicaragua,
Honduras, Costa Rica and Panama would not accept 'traders or
intellectuals'. The United States agreed to accept 27,370
immigrants annually. Only the Netherlands and Denmark
reflected a spirit of humanitarianism – their borders remained
open to those fleeing Germany.

Night and Fog   Anne refers to 'night and fog' and it becomes
a chant as the families are deported. Hitler's men trained

special troops to spirit people away so that their relatives, friends and neighbours did not know where they had gone – as if they had simply been swallowed up into the night. They called this policy 'Nacht und Nebel' (Night and Fog). Millions of people across Europe disappeared in this way.

The Allies   Otto Frank kept a map on a wall in the annex on which he charted the progress of the Allies and which maintained their hopes of liberation. Documentation now made public indicates that the Allied governments knew in some detail about the extermination camps. The moral responsibility for lack of action in the years leading up to and during the War may, in historical perspective, be shouldered by the many nations who did not open their frontiers to refugees from the Hitler regime whilst there was still time. The Swiss suggested to the Nazis that passports of Jews should be stamped with a letter J, so that they could be easily identified and sent back to Germany. In France and other occupied countries the police apparatus functioned as an efficient arm of the Gestapo. Even after the liberation of Rome in 1944, when half a million Hungarian Jews were still being deported to the gas chambers, the Pope did not raise his voice publicly against the crime, and no attempt was ever made to destroy the installations of Auschwitz; although their exact position and function were widely known. Not one statesman on the Allied side took a serious interest in the fate of the Jews because it seemed to have no significance to the outcome of the War.

Helping hands   This phrase is mentioned throughout the play and makes significant reference to the many thousands of non-Jewish people who put their own lives in danger to save others. They were, however, a minority and many Jews were betrayed by people who had taken them into hiding. Many people shut their eyes to what was happening. Pastor Niemoller, who was himself a victim of the Nazis, wrote eloquently about the silent bystander: 'First they came for the Jews and I did not speak out – because I was not a Jew. Then they came for the communists and I did not speak out – because I was not a communist. Then they came for the trade unionists and I did not speak out – because I was not a

trade unionist. Then they came for me – and there was no
one left to speak out for me.'

Dreams of Anne Frank   We know that Anne had a vivid
imagination and the writer uses this element of her character to
convey to us the frustrations, tensions and hopes that were part
of the two years existence in the Annex. We see things that
Anne was fond of (films, cartoons, dancing etc.) sometimes
distorted in her imagination to frightening nightmares. The
dreams portrayed in the play have within them a foretelling of
the future and we can see depicted the daily roll call in the
concentration camp ('no one is exempt'), the crematoria (the
gingerbread house), the labour camp (Snow White), Hitler's
death and Winston Churchill dispensing advice.

Wedding   In the play Anne dreams of getting married to Peter
and a traditional wedding is performed under the canopy
(chupa). The ceremony consists of blessings and responses and
the sharing of wine. The bridegroom smashes a glass after
which the couple are wished 'mazel tov' – good luck.

Liturgical music   Towards the end of the play you will hear a
song which begins with the words 'Ani Ma-amin' (I believe
with a perfect faith). These words were written about 800 years
ago by the doctor and philosopher Moses Maimonides who
condensed the precepts of the Jewish faith into thirteen
principles. During the War music was composed for it by the
fighters of the Warsaw Ghetto and this song became their
hymn. Anne translates the words of this song. It is followed by
a liturgical piece sung on the Day of Atonement – Shema
Kolenu (Hear our voice). This moving prayer was heard in the
concentration camps as six million Jews went to their deaths.

Hear our voice O Lord our God
Spare us and have pity on us
Accept our prayer with mercy and with favour
Turn us back O Lord unto yourself and we will gladly return
Renew our days as of old

Dreams of Anne Frank

a play for young people

for Erica

Dreams of Anne Frank was first produced at the Polka Theatre, London, on 3 October 1992, with the following cast of characters:

Otto Frank	Edward Halstead
Anne Frank	Elizabeth Chadwick
Edith Frank	Kitty Alvarez
Margot Frank	Celia Browning
Mrs Van Daan	Hollie Garrett
Mr Van Daan	Joe Cushley
Peter Van Daan	Tim Matthews
Mr Dussel	Brett Fancy

Directed by Leona Heimfeld
Designed by Fran Cooper
Music by David Burman

Setting

There is minimal scenery. Each scene is created by specific suggested images. There, but almost intangible, as if they might float away any moment (sometimes they do). This is to convey the fragility of the world around the players. A transient, temporary place they are just passing through. This is also to convey the fluidity of action, the dreams and imaginings of a young girl. The stage is uncluttered, except for a triangular pile of clothes, downstage off C, with Anne's diary on top of the pile. There is also an upturned chair. Another important feature of furniture on this sparse stage is a typical 1930s radiogram set. Apart from its usual function of being a conduit for the outside world – i.e. news bulletins and miscellaneous music programmes – it will also play gramophone records, the source of music that accompanies the songs in the play.

There is also a Helping Hand in this play: a hand at the door that from time to time delivers essentials.

Music for the play

Apart from the religious pieces and the occasional songs of the time, all the incidental music and songs can be specially composed for any specific production. The passage of time is a key theme in this play, and this can be reflected musically by repeated appearances of a plaintive motif which could be accompanied by a halting triplet rhythm on a solo piano. This can undergo several transformations as the play progresses; reflecting the changing moods and emotions of the characters. The songs are another important element; helping the essential expressionistic style of the text. The first song ('Yellow Star') can be based on a traditional Jewish mode and can sparingly interpolate the entire text, creating a coherent tapestry of sound, linking the two halves and helping to create the poignant and inexorable ending.

The house in which the Frank family hid.

Anne Frank. May 1940.

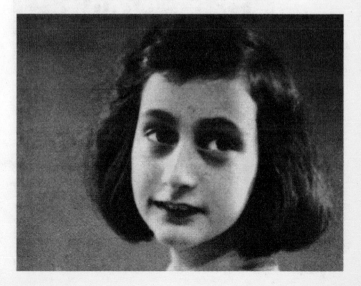

Nicola Buckingham as Anne Frank and Edward Halsted as Otto Frank.

Nicola Buckingham as Anne Frank.

Act One

Arrival

Scene One

Darkness.
A man enters. His clothes are formal. He is well dressed, spick
and span, almost out of keeping with the scene he has entered.
This is **Otto Frank**. *He lifts the diary from on top of the pile of*
clothes, and speaks quietly without undue emotion.

Otto I'm Otto Frank. Anne Frank was my daughter, and she
was very special. I survived the war. Somehow. Anne didn't.
Survival was random. Pure chance. That morning when our
liberators arrived, I just sat there. Numb. The gates were open
but I had no spirit to get up and run. I knew then that my wife
was dead, and my neighbours. And my children were God
knows where. I was breathing, yet I was dead. We were all
dead, those departed and those still there on that morning. The
gates were open and everything was incredibly silent and
peaceful. All the guards had disappeared; as if they had been
spirited away in the night, and that morning for the first time in
ages I heard a bird singing. I think it was a blackbird because
its song was so beautiful. It couldn't have been a nightingale.
They avoided the skies above Auschwitz. Then we heard the
sound of guns and great armoured vehicles on the move.
Getting closer. Russian soldiers appeared. With chocolate and
cigarettes, liniment and bandages. We didn't cheer. We just sat
there, slumped and staring. Nobody spoke. The sun was so
bright and the heat so soaked into my bones. And then one
soldier started to play his accordion. Suddenly someone danced.
In slow motion. Others joined in. More and more. Dancing.
Dancing. Soon, everyone who could stand on two legs was
dancing. And laughing. And crying. I watched. I just watched. I
loved my daughters. Margot and Anne. That goes without
saying. But Anne was special. She didn't survive the war. But

her words, her story, her secrets, her dreams are all here in this book. The diary of Anne Frank. (*He opens the diary.*)

The lights cross-fade, merging into the next scene.

Scene Two

Anne *appears, holding up a yellow star.*

Anne Morning star. Evening star. Yellow star Amsterdam. Nineteen forty-two. The German army occupies Holland. They have applied terrible rules that we must obey. Rules for Jews. That applies to me. 'Jews must wear a yellow star. Jews cannot go on trains. Jews must not drive. Jews cannot go shopping, except between three and five. Jews must only patronize Jewish shops.' We cannot go to the cinema, play tennis, go swimming. I cannot even go to the theatre. And now for the most frightening thing of all. They are beginning to round Jews up and take us away. Away from our homes, our beloved Amsterdam. A few days ago I celebrated my thirteenth birthday. My parents gave me this diary. It is my most precious possession. Yesterday I was just an ordinary girl living in Amsterdam. Today I am forced to wear this by our Nazi conquerors. Morning star, evening star, yellow star.

Scene Three

In their house the rest of the Frank family are celebrating their Sabbath. The candles are alight.

Anne It's the third of July. Nineteen forty-two. Mother's making havdala. Sabbath's over.

Edith *sings 'Eliyahoo Hanavi'.* **Otto**, **Margot** *and* **Anne** *join in the song.*

Edith (*singing*) 'We look forward to the coming of the Messiah and world peace.'

Anne Amen! Margot! We can play.

The tablecloth and candles go.

Hide and seek.

Margot Find me, Anne! Find me! You can't find me!

Anne *covers her eyes with her fingers.* **Margot** *darts around and hides.*

Anne (*finding* **Margot**) Got you.

Margot You cheated. You looked. Cheat! Cheat!

Anne Liar! Liar! My turn. My turn.

They continue playing and laughing. **Anne** *hides.*

My parents were folding sheets.

Otto *and* **Edith** *start folding sheets.*

It was Sunday. The fifth of July. The day after American Independence Day. My mother pretended she wasn't crying.

Edith Do you remember, Otto? One year ago today, exactly. We were boating on the River Amstel. Remember that beautiful picnic? The wine.

With the sheets, **Otto** *and* **Edith** *mime being on the boat.*

And that boat floating through that golden day.

Otto Yes, my love. And we shall go boating again, next year.

Anne Then Father made the announcement. I remember his exact words.

Otto Listen, children. Please. I must tell you something. We're going into hiding.

Anne Hiding? Great! They're joining in our game. You hide, Mother, with Margot. We'll find you.

The girls laugh.

Otto Be sensible, Anne. You know what I mean. We've been preparing for this for a long time. And now that time has come.

Edith We must be strong. And brave.

Anne When are we going into hiding?

Otto Thursday.

Anne Hurray!

Margot Hurray!

Margot *and* **Anne** *stand close, arms around each other.*

Anne Where are we going to hide?

Edith You'll find out soon enough.

Anne I was asking Daddy!

Margot Anne!

Anne Will we be all right?

Edith Of course, my love. We'll always be all right.

Otto There will be others hiding with us. The Van Daans.

Anne Who?

Edith You know the Van Daans. Their son Peter is about your age.

Anne I don't remember him.

Margot I do.

Anne Come on, Margot. Let's finish our game.

Edith Girls. No time to waste. Playtime's over.

Anne What do I leave behind? What can I take?

Otto Only necessary things.

Edith Absolute essentials.

Anne (*getting her satchel*) Essentials. My school satchel. I'm going to cram it full. Hair curlers.

Margot Really!

Anne Mind your own business, Margot! What are you taking?

Margot Absolute essentials.

Anne Handkerchiefs. School books. Film star photographs. Joan

Crawford. Bette Davis. Deanna Durbin. Mickey Rooney. Comb. Letters. Thousands of pencils. Elastic bands. My best book. *Emil and the Detectives*. Five pens. (*She smells a little bottle.*) Nice scent. Oh yes! Mustn't forget my new diary. Have you seen it? (*She has put all her things into her satchel but she has not included her diary.*) We're going into hiding. Going into hiding.

The others are all busy packing.

Four days later. It was Thursday, the ninth of July. I shall never forget that morning. It was raining. Imagine leaving your house, maybe forever.

Margot Anne. Please don't cry.

Anne I'm not! Liar! (*She's crying.*) I'm laughing. (*She laughs.*)

Margot You're mad.

Anne I must be mad to have you as a sister. Sorry, Margot. You're my favourite sister.

Margot Silly. I'm your only sister.

Anne Everyone says you're beautiful and intelligent. And I'm the cheeky one. But I don't mind, really. I'm brilliant.

Margot Exactly.

They laugh.

Anne I'm so happy. In hiding we no longer have to obey the Germans, the master race. No more dreaded rules for Jews.

Otto Girls!

Suddenly they are ready and all stand looking at the house.

Anne Goodbye, House.

House (**Edith**'s *taped voice*) So, you're leaving. How could you do this to me?

Anne Sorry. It wasn't us.

House I know. I'll miss you all.

Anne We'll always remember you.

House And I'll always hear you. I have your laughter, your singing, soaked in my walls, echoing forever.

We hear laughter and singing.

Goodbye, Frank family.

Anne House! Don't cry.

House I'll try.

Anne Thank you for everything. My brain is at a fairground, on the roller coaster. Up and down. Happy. Sad. Afraid. Excited. My emotions are racing. My imagination spilling over. After all, I am a creative artist. I'm going to be a writer when this war is over.

The other three wait as she lingers.

Edith Anne!

Margot We're waiting.

Anne Imagine leaving your house, forever.

They are all about to go.

Diary! Can't go without my diary. (*She takes up the diary and opens it.*)

Diary Hello, Anne.

Anne Hello, Diary.

Diary Nothing entered in me yet. Your world is a fresh clean page.

Anne Marvellous.

Diary Anne! Remember, even if you are locked away, all is possible in your head.

Anne (*taking up the diary's speech*) You can be trapped in a box, or in sadness, but you travel in your mind. You can be imprisoned in a basement or an attic, but you can go anywhere. In your dreams you are free, the past, the present, the future. It is all open to you within my pages. Use me well. (*As herself.*) I promise. I shall write everything down. Everything. Thoughts. Events. Dreams.

Diary That's what I'm here for.

Anne I shall confide my secrets. Only to you.

Diary Whatever you write is safe with me. No one else will ever know. It's our secret.

Anne Yes. Forever. (*Clutching her diary close.*) Let's go.

Margot What's that?

Anne My diary.

Margot Why are you holding it so close? Is it that precious?

Anne I couldn't survive without my diary.

Edith Come on.

Otto, **Edith** *and* **Margot** *leave.* **Anne** *sings.*

Anne from Amsterdam

Anne   Fate gave me a yellow star.
A badge to tell them who I am.
I'm Anne from Amsterdam.
I'm Anne Frank and I'm a Jew.
And I'm the same as you and you.
Or you and you and you.
But fate gave me the yellow star.
Yellow star.
The star's to put me in my place,
To wear it as the badge of shame,
But I'm Anne from Amsterdam.
I'm proud of who I am.
We have to hide away from light
Because they come for us at night.
And pack us off to God knows where,
And all we have is where we are.
But fate gave me the yellow star.
Yellow star.

Scene Four

The Frank family arrive in the attic, carrying boxes, cases and blankets. First they explore the dimensions of their hiding-place.

Otto This attic. Our secret hiding-place.

Margot It's very small.

Anne It's very large.

Margot Anne! Your imagination! Come down to earth for once.

Anne (*at the window*) Look down there. That's earth. It's not such a nice place to be at this moment. I'm sleeping up there! Right! Everything's settled. I feel so, so happy. Be happy. Please.

Margot I'll try.

Anne Are you depressed?

Margot I'm all right. When I do get depressed your spirit lifts me. But I do wish those other people would arrive. I believe the boy's name is Peter. How old is he?

Anne Who cares? What would you like to do more than anything else in the world?

Margot Go ice-skating.

Anne Listen! We are cooped up here and we can go nowhere. Therefore – we can go everywhere. In captivity you can be free inside your head. (*She orders up a scene.*) Ebony-black, mauve sky. Shivering silver moon. Frozen-over, vast expanse of lake. Shimmering, diamond sheet of ice. There! It's all yours.

Margot Can I? Are you sure?

Anne Absolutely! If you really want to. Use your imagination and it's all yours. Go on! What are you waiting for?

Margot *goes skating on the frozen lake.*

Margot It's wonderful! I'm skating. I'm skating. Join me! Join me!

Anne *joins her and soon they are both skating and laughing joyously. But then* **Anne** *suddenly stops.*

Spoilsport! What's wrong?

Anne Someone walked over my grave.

Anne *switches on the radio and twiddles the dial. A victory 'V' drumbeat is heard.*

Announcer's voice This is the BBC in London calling Europe. We now present Carrol Gibbons and his dance band from the Savoy Hotel. In the heart of London.

The music continues softly in the background. **Margot** *and* **Anne** *playfully dance together as they put things away. They laugh. There is a noise outside. The family freeze with fear.*

Margot Are we betrayed?

Otto Leave it to me. (*He cautiously listens at the trapdoor.*)

Scene Five

Otto *opens the trapdoor. Outside we hear a woman laughing, raucously.*

Otto It's all right. It's the Van Daans.

Much relief.

Edith Thank God. Now don't forget, girls, let them settle in. Don't intrude.

The **Van Daans** *enter with their belongings. They try to be quiet but are very loud.*

Mr Van Daan ⎫
Mrs Van Daan ⎭ (*together*) We're the Van Daans.

Edith Ah! The Van Daans!

Mrs Van Daan (*booming voice, laughing*) I'm Mrs Van Daan. We're so happy to be here. This is my husband.

Mr Van Daan How do you do.

Mrs Van Daan And this is my son, Peter.

Franks How do you do.

Anne (*gently mocking*) How do you do. How do you do.

Mr Van Daan Yes. Thank God at last we're safe and secure.

Edith What's it like outside?

Mr Van Daan Let us change the subject. Please.

Mrs Van Daan (*ignoring the plea*) It's terrible out there. It breaks my heart.

Mr Van Daan The Germans are doing exactly what they promised. After all it's all there in *Mein Kampf* and the Nuremberg Laws.

Mrs Van Daan Since you went into hiding it's got much worse, I can tell you. Every day worse and worse. They're dragging people off the street, from their beds. I saw them on the other side of the road this morning, carrying an old man out.

Mr Van Daan Please. Can we change the subject?

Mrs Van Daan Mr Levene, ninety-two years old, too crippled to walk, they carried him out and threw him into a truck, like a sack of potatoes.

Margot Where did they take him?

Edith God knows where. God rest his soul.

Otto Please. We must now concentrate on us. On how we can all live together in harmony.

Mr Van Daan Absolutely.

Mrs Van Daan (*grabbing a chair and sitting down*) I like this chair. It's perfect for my back.

Anne I'm sorry; that's my chair.

Mr Van Daan Your chair? Ha! Ha! Ha! That's funny.

Anne It's my chair! My chair! It's mine.

Mrs Van Daan I see. And does it have your name on it?

Edith Sarcasm is the lowest form of wit.

Margot Exactly.

Anne I want my chair. Give it to me.

Mrs Van Daan It's mine. How dare you?

They struggle for the chair.

Edith Anne! Behave!

Mrs Van Daan Yes. Respect your elders.

Anne If you were respectable, I would.

Edith Anne! I won't tell you again.

Otto Please. This is absurd.

Mr Van Daan Absolutely. How right you are, Mr Frank.

Otto We must behave reasonably. If we balance things out inside, we may be able to survive when we finally go out. May we show you around?

Mrs Van Daan That would be very nice.

Otto I've got it all sorted. Come. Everything should work very well if we obey certain rules.

Edith And if we are all tolerant of each other and understanding.

Mrs Van Daan Hear! Hear!

Mr Van Daan You echo my sentiments entirely.

The four adults leave to look round the attic. The three young people remain and at first are silent and embarrassed.

Margot Hello, Peter.

Anne Why are you saying hello? We've said hello already.

Margot How old are you?

Peter Why do you want to know?

Margot No reason.

Peter I'm fifteen. How old are you?

Margot Why do you want to know?

Peter No reason.

Margot I'm sixteen.

Edith Margot! Would you come here, please?

Margot Yes, Mother. (*She joins the adults.*)

Peter How old are you?

Anne Why do you want to know?

Peter No reason.

The others return and start to unpack. **Mrs Van Daan** *drops an iron on the floor.*

Mr Van Daan Clumsy wumsy.

Otto We must remember to be quiet. There are people right below us who don't even know we're here.

Anne Yes. We must have hush.

Margot And shush.

Peter Sneezing is not allowed. Excuse me. Atishoo.

Anne Hiccups are not allowed. (*She hiccups.*) 'Scuse me.

Margot Nor snoring (*She snores.*)

Anne Nor coughing.

Peter Nor talking in your sleep.

Margot Nor the belly grumbles.

Anne Nor heaving. Nor breathing. Nor crying. Nor dying.

Throughout this, **Anne** *and* **Margot** *pick on* **Peter***, till finally he falls over.*

Edith Anne!

Mr Van Daan Mrs Frank, don't worry. It's nice they're getting on so well. And us.

Edith We have to. After all, this one little attic is our whole world, from now on. God help us.

Mr Van Daan He will. I told you I had a little chat with him last night.

Peter Dad!

Mrs Van Daan Isn't he funny? Isn't he lovely? (*She pinches his cheek.*) Ooh! I could eat him.

Mr Van Daan Delicious! Delilah!

Mrs Van Daan Mr and Mrs Frank, I would just like you to know that you will find us totally co-operative. I couldn't wish to hide with nicer people.

Mrs Van Daan *does not notice that* **Anne** *is wickedly aping her words.*

And you will find us equally nice and responsible. You will also find that I am a modest person. A modest, humble and quiet person. Humble and unassuming. Courteous. Gracious. Polite. Self-effacing. Nice. Decent. Pleasant. Gentle. Spick and span. Affable. And unpretentious. And harmless. Inoffensive. Well mannered. Conciliatory. Sociable. Friendly. Civil. Dignified. Unimposing. Shy. Retiring. Reserved. Almost bashful. In other words, I know my place and I never fuss. (*She spins round and discovers* **Anne** *mimicking her.*) How dare you! How dare you!

Edith She's only a child. She didn't mean anything.

Mrs Van Daan If she was only my child I would scold her.

Edith Apologize.

Anne I'm sorry.

Mrs Van Daan You're a spoiled brat. A monster.

Edith Please do not call my child a monster.

Mrs Van Daan I will if she behaves monstrously.

Edith You are an impossible woman.

Mrs Van Daan What? Me? I am the most possible person you could ever come across.

Mr Van Daan Let's all play cards. Yes? Wonderful!

Otto *and* **Edith** *look pained, but she nods. They all sit down.*

Rummy?

They play cards. **Margot** *looks at* **Peter**, *who looks at* **Anne**. **Anne** *goes to the window. There she sees light and dark.*

Anne Days pass, nights pass. Nothing happens. That's life. Passing before your eyes. And if you write about it, record it, at least you have proof it was there. It's all in the words.

There is a sudden knocking on the trapdoor.

Margot (*rushing to* **Edith**) Are we betrayed?

Silence for a long moment.

Otto Leave this to me.

He goes to the trapdoor and listens.

Scene Six

Otto *opens the trapdoor and is handed a birthday cake.*

Anne It's a gift from helping hands. Peter! Here's your cake.

Peter Cake? Is it my birthday already?

Margot Of course it's your birthday, silly. As if you didn't know.

Mr Van Daan Cake? How have I survived without cake?

They all sing 'Happy Birthday'.

(*Cutting the cake.*) Here! Shove this in your cakehole, darling.

Margot What can I get you for your birthday?

Peter The Eiffel Tower.

Margot OK. I'll wrap it up tomorrow morning.

Mrs Van Daan How do we know we can trust those helping hands?

Otto They've proved themselves, these Dutch Christians.

Mrs Van Daan I trust no one.

Otto We have no choice. We are in their hands.

Edith If they're caught helping us, it's certain death. They're very brave. I wonder whether I would do the same for them if they were in our position.

They all go silent.

Anne Do you like him?

Margot Who?

Anne Peter.

Margot Not much. A bit, maybe.

Sirens sound.

Anne They're bombing Amsterdam again. Look! Look at the sky! The tracery is so beautiful.

The sound of bombs falling.

Otto Anne! Come away from that window.

Mrs Van Daan Peter!

Otto Please!

Edith Anne! Margot! Come here, darling.

Margot *goes to her mother.*

Mr Van Daan Are you scared, blossom?

Mrs Van Daan You kidding? With my caveman beside me?

Otto The more the British bomb, the better. I rejoice every time the RAF are overhead.

Edith As long as we all don't die in the process.

Mr Van Daan (*singing to 'Coming Round the Mountain'*) 'Oh we'll all go together when we go – '

Anne My beloved Amsterdam.

Otto (*joining* **Anne**) Come bombs, give those Nazis hell. (*He cuddles his daughter as the bombs come closer and closer.*)

Mrs Van Daan We have to have faith, Mrs Frank.

Edith Yes. If only there was a shop where we could buy some.

Mr Van Daan Mr Frank! Let's get on with the game.

Otto *returns to the game. The all-clear sounds. Day and night and day again outside.*

Anne All clear! The best sound in the world. I long to hear it. Yet I want them beaten. Day after day after day the same. Playing cards. Sleeping. Getting up. Morning always brings breakfast. And fresh hope. It's morning, everyone!

All Morning?

Mrs Van Daan Gosh! Time just flies. Life! Grab it while you can.

Her husband grabs her. She laughs. They all leave their card game.

Edith Breakfast, everyone. Come and get it.

Mr Van Daan (*impersonating Billy Cotton from 'Billy Cotton's Band Show'*) Wakey! Wakey! Come and get it.

He sings a couple of lines from 'Somebody Stole My Girl'; cuddling his giggling wife and pulling her out of sight.

Anne I love early morning. Maybe today the war will be over. If wishes could fly all my hopes would hold up the sky. Miracles, like everything else, are in short supply these days. Listen! I can hear the beautiful song of a blackbird. And children, in a school playground. If only I could be at school, playing with my friends. Will I ever see them again?

Margot What's the time?

Anne You mean, what is time? It's half-past forever. Twenty past never.

There is a sudden knock on the trapdoor.

It's something nice again, I'm sure.

Otto Someone to tell us the war is over.

Mrs Van Daan Some French perfume.

Edith A new hat. Elegant. Stunning.

Mr Van Daan A joke book, chock-a-block with howlers.

Margot A fluffy Persian kitten.

Peter Chocolate éclairs. A bowl of hot custard.

They all rush to the trapdoor, just as **Otto** *opens it.*

Scene Seven

Dussel *enters.*

Dussel (*giving* **Otto** *his card*) Mr Dussel, at your service. You have been expecting me.

Otto Yes, we were alerted that you would possibly be joining us in our hiding-place. I'm Otto Frank. This is my wife and my two daughters.

They shake hands.

Mrs Van Daan How do you do. We haven't been introduced.

Dussel What nice, glistening teeth you have. I can see they are all your own.

Mr Van Daan I didn't quite catch your name.

Dussel *sings.*

Dussel the Dentist

Dussel   I'm Dussel the dentist, seeker-out of cavities.
Not caring for your teeth is one of life's depravities
Keeping them clean and free of goo
Is the only thing that should matter to you.
I'm Dussel the dentist, seeker-out of cavities.
Not caring for your teeth is one of life's depravities.
So you can expect me every morning, without warning,
   every morning, without warning,
To stab and to poke for bacterial decay.
So come, my friends, without delay.
No time to be lost,
Just bend to my will
I'll solve all your problems with my probe and my drill.
Probe and drill! And probe and drill and probe and
   drill.
And probe and drill.
I'm Dussel the dentist, seeker-out of cavities.
Not caring for your teeth is one of life's depravities
Keeping them clean and free of goo
Is the only thing that should matter to you.

(*Speaking.*) Right! Line up. Open wide!

Everyone is petrified. They line themselves up like frightened soldiers, but **Peter** *and* **Margot** *giggle.*

Silence! This is not to be enjoyed. (*He is about to probe into* **Mrs Van Daan**'s *mouth.*) Wait! Someone's missing! Someone is disobeying the rules.

Mrs Van Daan It's her over there. Saint Anne of Amsterdam.

Dussel Why is she staring into space?

Peter She's writing a book about the human race.

Mr Van Daan She thinks it makes her special.

Dussel No one is exempt. Call her over here.

Margot Leave her alone. She's just writing.

Peter She's writing all this. Writing all us.

Mrs Van Daan She's never really with us.

Dussel Well, I personally refuse to be written about. Where was I? Oh yes! You! (*He now probes deep into* **Mrs Van Daan**'s *mouth.*) Nasty! My God! Nasty! Nasty!

The woman lets out a piercing scream.

Anne (*wickedly*) Ssshuusshhh!

Anne *laughs from her distance. They are back down to earth.*

Mrs Van Daan Nasty girl! Come down to earth.

Edith What's it like out there?

Otto Darling.

Mrs Van Daan Look at his eyes. It's terrible. Tell us.

Mr Van Daan Precious! If the world's coming to an end, why broadcast it?

Mrs Van Daan Listen.

Dussel It was the middle of the night. I heard a scream. I saw the family next door being dragged out. I thought it was a dream. It was all in slow motion. The baby cried. The mother tried to keep her quiet. The soldiers kept hitting, hitting with their guns. The child went silent. I couldn't look any more.

Edith Things have gone from bad to worse since we went into hiding.

Peter We should have made a stand. We should have died fighting.

Otto What? Us? Against the whole German army?

Dussel Incidentally, where do I sleep?

Otto Over there. Up near Anne.

Anne Oh no!

Dussel (*muttering*) I see. Still, could be worse. Plenty of mouths to work upon up here. We must surgery on. (*He unpacks his things.*)

Anne You see, Peter, time is a mystery. What has happened is happening again. What is about to happen has happened before. Sleep is the only thing that separates yesterday from tomorrow. Memory has no continuity. Thoughts, like a jigsaw, are all over the place.

Peter I see. (*He doesn't.*)

Margot I don't either.

Mrs Van Daan If I had daughters, they would be helping.

Margot (*going to the women*) May I help you with dinner?

Mrs Van Daan What a good girl.

Mr Van Daan Hmmmm! Something smells good. What's for supper, precious?

Mrs Van Daan Me.

Mr Van Daan Hmmm! Yummy. Yummy.

Edith It's amazing. It seems we've only just got up, yet it's evening already and we're about to have dinner. Time flies.

Mrs Van Daan Come and get it. Lovely grub.

Peter Great. Starving.

Margot What is it?

Anne What else. Potatoes and cabbage.

Peter Boiled together, as usual.

Anne How did you guess?

Edith Dig in.

They all eat.

Mrs Van Daan Lovely to see a man with a healthy appetite.

Mr Van Daan You said it. What I wouldn't do for a nice slice of cow.

Anne Help yourself! Eat your wife!

Anne *points at* **Mrs Van Daan**, *who hasn't heard. The others splutter and laugh.*

Edith Anne!

Mrs Van Daan What did she say?

Mr Van Daan Nothing, sweetheart. You know, I've been thinking. If God lived on earth we'd all break his windows.

Mrs Van Daan Listen, young lady, I know you said something nasty about me. You're rude and ill-mannered.

Edith Apologize!

Anne You have to dream to get away. Just think of it. Imagine being locked away, in an attic with seven others, day after day. The noises they make, the games they play. You have to dream to get away. Just think of it. The way they sit, the way they smell, their rumbling tummies could make life hell. How I wish I could live in a shell. Just think of it. To get away, to get away from these same old faces that get in the way. These people I'm trapped with day after day. You have to dream to get away. Or lose yourself in French verbs.

Anne *takes up an exercise book and writes in it.* **Peter** *hovers.*

Peter What are you doing now?

Anne Mustn't fall behind.

Peter With what?

Anne Lessons.

Peter What sort of lessons?

Anne French! If you really must know.

Peter I speak French.

Anne Really? Say something.

Peter *Je vous aime.*

Anne *laughs.*

What's wrong?

Anne If you really loved someone you should say: *Je t'aime.*

Peter You obviously know more than me. (*Nervous.*) I – I know! Why don't we do schoolwork together?

Anne No, thank you.

Peter Sorry. Excuse me for breathing. (*He retreats.*)

Mr Van Daan Once upon a time there was a man who told jokes all the time. (*He is laughing already.*) Stop me if you've heard this –

The children groan.

Margot Please excuse me. (*She leaves the table.*)

Peter Please excuse me. (*He leaves the table.*)

Anne *leaves the table and brushes* **Margot***'s hair.* **Peter** *watches them.*

Anne I wish you wouldn't watch me all the time.

Scene Eight

Anne *goes to the radio and twiddles the knob. There is interference.*

Announcer This is the BBC Home Service. Calling Europe. We bring you the Prime Minister of Great Britain, Mr Winston Churchill.

Anne Good evening, Mr Churchill.

Churchill Good evening, Anne. You sound troubled.

Anne It's just that I would like to tell your Air Force to drop more bombs on Amsterdam. But tell them to take care to only bomb the Nazis and not our beautiful city or the Dutch people in their air-raid shelters or people like us, in hiding.

Churchill I'll do my best.

Anne Thank you.

Churchill I believe you are writing a diary, Anne?

Anne Yes, Mr Churchill.

Churchill Keep up the good work.

Anne I shall.

Churchill Take care of yourself and don't catch cold.

Anne Thank you, sir.

Churchill Not at all. And now I would like to say a few words to the others. Good night.

Anne Good night.

Otto Anne! Can you please stop talking to yourself.

Anne I was talking to Mr Churchill.

Otto Yes. Of course you were.

Anne He wants to say something to all of you.

Announcer This is the BBC Home Service. Calling Europe. We bring you the Prime Minister of Great Britain, Mr Winston Churchill.

Otto It is him.

They huddle round the radiogram.

Churchill This is not the end, not even the beginning of the end. But it is the end of the beginning.

An air-raid siren sounds and we hear the crump of bombs. The others seem suddenly dispirited.

Anne I wish this day was over.

It gradually gets dark.

Nightfall! Look! Suddenly you notice it.

They all start to make ready for bed.

And once again another deadly symphony begins.

The bombs whistle down. The place shakes. Everyone freezes with fear as the bombs come close.

But I also love the night. I watch them come and go. Again and again. Thankful that tomorrow will come sooner. And the end of the war. And freedom. Oh God, how long can we survive here?

Churchill Anne! Be brave. Be strong.

Anne Thank you, Mr Churchill.

Scene Nine

Mrs Van Daan Bedtime already? Surely we only just got up?

Everyone starts washing and gargling.

Edith You're right. There doesn't seem to be enough time for anything.

Mr Van Daan But you've always got time to go to your own funeral.

Mrs Van Daan Treasure? Why so morbid?

Mr Van Daan Sorry, poppet. I've always got time for you.

Otto This is the end of the beginning.

Edith But surely it's the beginning of the end of the middle.

Mrs Van Daan No. The beginning of the middle of the end.

Dussel More like the middle of the beginning of the end.

Mrs Van Daan That means it's the beginning of the end! In that case the war's almost over. We're going to survive.

Otto Listen! Everyone. You heard what Winston Churchill said. It's only the end of the beginning.

Edith There's still a long way to go.

On the radio Vera Lynn sings 'Silver Wings in the Moonlight'.

Margot How will we be able to survive this?

Edith We are a nation of survivors. We crossed the desert.

Mrs Van Daan We should have stayed on the other side.

Dussel We are Jews. We endure.

Margot We are Dutch. Almost.

Dussel We survived the wilderness. With all teeth intact.

Margot We will survive all this, won't we, Anne? Anne? Tell me if you know.

Anne Don't worry. In my diary people and humanity and good and justice will triumph over evil. In my diary I know we are all safe and we shall all be saved.

Mrs Van Daan That diary is not the world.

Anne It is my world. (*She makes an entry into the diary.*)

Otto That diary might be our witness. Who knows? It could warn the world not to fall into the dark again.

Dussel I want to survive. Here and now. Not in words.

Mrs Van Daan Damn the diary. I'm going to bed.

Otto Look at my daughter. She's dreaming again.

Edith Remember, Otto, all those years ago. Before we had kids. And we went on holiday to Berlin.

Otto I remember.

Edith And all the leaves were bursting green along the Unter den Linden. And everyone was laughing. And later we went boating on Lake Wansee. You were so gallant, so handsome. You still are.

Otto Thank you, my love. You had such a pretty dress on. A sort of golden yellow. You were so beautiful. You still are.

Anne *yawns.*

Edith Go to bed!

Anne Yes, Mother. Soon.

Anne *makes an entry in her diary and bumps into a shirtless* **Peter** *who has been washing himself and hovering.*

Showing off again.

Peter Showing off?

Anne If I had a body like that, I wouldn't show it off.

Peter You never talk to me properly. Why don't you like me?

Silence.

Can I see your diary?

Silence.

Am I in it?

Silence.

I'm intrigued.

Anne Look, Peter! Because we live in close proximity, we do not actually need to like each other. Or be involved in any way.

Peter I agree. Good night.

Anne Good night.

Mrs Van Daan (*seeing them*) Peter! Bedtime!

Peter Yes, Mother. Good night.

Anne You've said it already.

Edith I won't tell you again.

Anne Sorry, Mother. Just coming. Peter is not very good-looking. But he has such lovely eyes.

Edith Anne!

Anne Coming! (*But she does not go to bed.*) Funny thing, freedom. You take it for granted until you lose it.

Otto (*mumbling from sleep*) Anne! Put away that diary and go to bed.

Anne Yes, Father. Soon.

Margot (*calling across in a whisper*) Anne! You awake?

Anne No!

Margot Me also. I miss the snow. Being able to walk through snow.

Anne In my dreams I'm wandering through the softest, purest, finest snow you ever saw.

The visual effect is immediate.

Margot Thank you. I can see it. Good night, Anne darling.

Anne Good night, Margot.

They settle down. But in the dark **Anne** *cries.*

Edith (*going to* **Anne**) There! There! My little darling! Everything will be all right! My lovely girl. I can still see you both when you were very small, and I can hear you, giggling in the golden sunlight, building castles upon the sand banks of time. You both wore beautiful white dresses and gorgeous floppy hats. And we took you both to Berlin long before you-know-who came to power. We sat outside a café in the Unter den Linden, just watching the passers-by. Somehow or other it seems like another universe. Unter den Linden. Under the Lime Trees. Mad, audacious Berlin. Such a beautiful city. City of chestnut blossom. And not a slogan, not a murderous look in sight. (*She almost cries.*)

Anne (*comforting her*) Thank you, Mother, for being you.

Edith *kisses* **Anne** *and goes back to bed.*

Edith Good night.

Helping Hand

(Singing.)   Helping Hand,
                      Please help me.
                      Knock on my door,
                      Bring me good news.

Margot   Helping Hand,
                      Please help me.
                      Bring me some hope,
                      Open the way.

Mrs Van Daan   Unlock this dark,
                      Throw away hate.

Peter   Helping Hand,
                      Please help me.
                      Hold the torch high.
                      Save us in time.

Mr Van Daan   Touch people's hearts,
                      Turn on their love.

Dussel   Take up the sword,
                      Slash away cloud.

There is a sudden noise outside and a crash. They all freeze.

Margot Are we betrayed?

Otto Leave this to me.

Otto *opens the trapdoor and disappears. He returns relieved.*

A cat. Just a mangy old tomcat, on the prowl, looking for his girlfriend.

Relief. Reprise of 'Helping Hand'.

(Singing.)   Helping Hand,
                      Please help us.
                      Bring the world peace.
                      Bring the world peace.

Anne   Helping Hand,
                 Please help me.

Curtain.

Act Two

Departure

Scene One

The cast enter and assemble as if asleep. Music starts and one by one they begin dancing.

Otto *enters with the diary and puts it down.*

The music stops.

Scene Two

Anne (*clutching her diary*) August the fourth. Nineteen forty-four. The war is almost over and Germany is losing. The end cannot be that far away.

Margot It wouldn't be a bad idea if you gave us a helping hand, sometimes.

Mrs Van Daan Hear! Hear!

Peter (*exercising*) Ann works harder than all of us. In her mind.

Mr Van Daan Yes. Leave her alone. She's only a child. What does she know of the world.

Dussel I don't object to her diary, as long as it is rational, truthful and objective.

Anne Truth is never objective. We all have our own version. If you wore a hat, I would say you are talking out of it.

Mrs Van Daan How could you allow her to speak like that to you?

Anne Thus another day passes. And another day. Days merge into days. A daze of days. No real signposts. Just days and days and days.

Mr Van Daan Would like to hear a joke?

Dussel No thank you.

Mr Van Daan It'll kill you. Hitler was on his horse, riding down the centre of Berlin, his legions behind him. The horse slipped and Hitler fell off and would have fallen on his head and probably died of a brain injury, if a little man on the pavement hadn't rushed forward and somehow bravely managed to break Der Führer's fall. 'How can I thank you?' Hitler said. 'What is your name?' The little man replied, 'Solomon Cohen.' Hitler was surprised. 'But you're a Jew!' 'What else?' said the little man. 'Never mind,' Hitler said, 'you acted with extreme courage and I would like to grant you anything you desire. Anything.' The man thought for a moment. 'Anything? Please! Not a word of this to anyone.'

Nobody laughs.

Isn't that fantastically funny?

Again he meets with a blank response.

I can sing too. I'm as good as Eddie Cantor or Al Jolson, even if I do say so myself. Listen. (*He gets down on one knee.*) 'Climb upon my knee, Sonny Boy, though you're sixty-three, Sonny Boy.'

Mrs Van Daan Eat breakfast. It's getting cold.

Peter (*joining* **Anne**) You are the watcher. The witness.

Anne Writing helps me pass the time. It gives me a purpose. It's everything.

Peter *and* **Anne** *sing.*

> *When the War Is Over*

Peter   When the war is over
      We'll fly to Samarkand
      And cross the Gobi desert
      Find treasure in the sand.

Anne   When the war is over
      I'll rush out in the street

> And chat with everybody
> And life will be complete.

Peter When the war is over
We'll drive to Kathmandu
And swim in coral oceans,
Climb pyramids in Peru.

Anne When the war is over
I'll just walk in the rain,
Eat a toffee apple,
See my house again.

Peter When the war is over
We'll climb Mount Everest
And then fly off to Africa
Our lives an endless quest.

Anne When the war is over
I'll paddle in the sea
Licking chocolate ice-cream
And have my friends to tea.

Both When the war is over
And niceness is the rule
We'll get our books together
And then we'll go to school.

> When the war is over,
> When the war is over,
> When the war is over,
> When the war is over.

Peter You never stop. What is there to write about?

Anne The diary opens my mind. I can explore myself. My hidden self. I remove myself from monotony. I can dream. Let's go.

Peter Where?

Anne Quickly! Hop aboard my dream.

Peter I'm there already.

Scene Three

In the Black Forest.

Anne Why does everyone always pick on me? If I'm silent, I'm sulking. If I'm writing, I'm being aloof, mysterious. If I talk, I'm cheeky. They say I cause all the trouble. But I'm never, never to blame.

Peter Never! We're in a forest.

Anne In the forest of my brain. Who am I? Which way did I go? I don't know who I am.

Peter If I kiss you you'll know who you are.

Anne Ssssh. This is the Black Forest where good German folk live. Slowly. We mustn't kill crocuses. Stop a moment. Don't you love spring? Tiny flowers; peeping through the hard earth. Each one a miracle. Yellow, mauve crocus. Snowdrop. Primrose. Violet. And look! Trees are more beautiful than people. No! That's not true. People are the most beautiful things in the whole of creation. Why have you stopped walking?

Peter What are we doing in the Black Forest?

Anne What are we doing in life? Creep!

Peter I'm not a creep. I'm very nice. Taste me.

Anne We must be careful or the witch will get us.

Peter Let me put my arm around you?

Anne I prefer the witch.

Peter Do you like me?

Anne Not much.

Peter That makes two of us. Goodbye.

Peter *goes.*

Anne I was only joking. Come back. Please! I wish he'd come back. He's got such a nice smile. Why are boys so stupid? I don't like being alone.

Mrs Van Daan *enters.*

Mrs Van Daan (*as a witch, wearing a potty on her head*) You're not alone. Welcome to my gingerbread house.

A gingerbread house appears.

Anne How beautiful. It smells so fresh. It's still warm. May I go inside?

Mrs Van Daan It's all yours.

Anne *enters the house.*

Anne It's very hot in here. Are you coming in?

Mrs Van Daan Presently.

Anne May I come out now?

Mrs Van Daan No. Stay. You are the chosen. You'll get used to it.

Anne I'm afraid and hungry.

Mrs Van Daan Then eat the house.

Anne Thank you! Can I eat the doorknob?

Mrs Van Daan Be my guest. Lick the mirror. It's honey toffee.

Anne *starts to eat.*

There's the oven over there. Where it all happens.

Anne Yum. Yum.

Mrs Van Daan What are you writing, Anne, all the time?

Anne Words. Just words.

Mrs Van Daan A great epic, I'm sure. You might become famous. The world at your feet.

Anne Poor world. I wouldn't like to be at my feet.

Mrs Van Daan But none of us will know, of course.

Anne I know. How sad.

Mrs Van Daan How old are you?

Anne Funny, you're a witch, but I'm not afraid of you. I'm fourteen.

Mrs Van Daan What would you like more than anything else in the world?

Anne To be fifteen. To be ordinary. To live a quiet life. To be famous. To go everywhere. I'm confused. Strange things are happening inside me. You see, I want to grow up.

Mrs Van Daan Well, eat then. You couldn't have come to a better place. Nothing like a gingerbread house to clear up confusion. This oven solves everything. The best German firms tendered for it and it's very efficient. Eat! Eat! There's lots of Jews waiting to be admitted. Gingerbread and hard work makes free. Look! Maybe they can help you.

Edith, Margot, Otto, Mr Van Daan *and* **Dussel** *enter.*

Anne Mother! Margot! (*She cuddles them.*)

Margot What are you doing?

Anne Eating this gingerbread house, of course.

Dussel May we join you?

Anne Be my guest.

Edith Dig in, everyone. It's not rationed. Enjoy.

Mr Van Daan I'm famished.

Otto Sweet for the sweet.

They get on all fours and ravenously start to eat the house.

Edith Where are we?

Anne The enchanted forest. Where you meet yourself and come face to face with your future. Where's Peter?

Peter *enters.*

Peter I love you. I am death. And you are mine. Forever. Come.

Anne Help me! Help me!

Everyone sings 'Who's Afraid of the Big, Bad Wolf'.

Scene Four

Margot Thank you, thank you. And now we bring you the Andrews Sisters!

Margot, Edith *and* **Mrs Van Daan** *sing.*

Margot
Edith   } Mother, may I go out dancing?
Mrs Van Daan Yes, my darling daughter.
Mother, may I try romancing?
Yes, my darling daughter.
What if there's a moon, Mother darling,
And it's shining on the water?
Mother, should I keep on dancing?
Yes, my darling daughter –

Anne *screams.*

Anne *Help me! Help me! Mother! Help me!*

Edith (*rushing to her*) Anne! Darling!

Anne Where am I?

Edith Having a nasty nightmare. You're all right.

Anne Please go back to the others.

Edith You sure? (**Edith** *returns to the others. They all play cards.*)

Anne Peter, I ran away from you. But when you weren't there I looked for you.

Peter The things you run away from, you run right into.

Anti-aircraft shells and bomb sounds reverberate.

Anne The war outside is going well.

Peter Yes. It will all be over soon.

Anne (*shivering*) I'm scared.

Peter We're all scared. We have a right to be. I like you, a lot.

Anne I know.

Peter I like you very much. Anne. Say something.

Anne The war will be over soon.

Peter I don't ever want another girlfriend.

Anne Oh?

Peter You've got plenty of words for your diary, but so few for me.

Anne Jealous?

Peter Yes.

Anne You've got very nice eyes.

Peter You think so? I – I lo – like you.

Anne Good.

Peter Did you say 'Good'? (*He turns cartwheels.*)

Anne Quiet! Keep it secret.

He is about to kiss her, but at the last moment lacks the courage.

Mrs Van Daan (*calling*) Peter!

Peter If only we could escape. For always.

Anne *searches for a doll.*

Anne (*finding it*) Margaret! There you are! Where have you been, you naughty girl? (*She holds the doll very tight.*) Sad, really. Suddenly I'm too old for you. And I'm too young for babies.

Otto (*touching her very gently*) You all right?

Anne I'm fine.

Otto Don't worry, my darling. Everything's all right. You were just having a bad dream.

Anne I know. I was so afraid in that dream. I was looking everywhere for my lost childhood. I hate being shut up here. But I must write. And I must dream.

Otto Is this all a dream?

Anne Yes.

Otto Then dream this. Your mother and I care for you so much, now and forever, even in the darkest corners of your dream.

Anne Thank you.

Otto Tell you what isn't a dream. The fact that you are special. And something wonderful will happen to you.

Anne What do you mean?

Otto I'm not sure. There's no logic in faith. But we're all going to be so proud of you.

Anne What will we do after the war?

Otto First we'll go on holiday. To the coast. To Blankenberg. Or maybe to Paris or London and see all the sights. Big Ben. Buckingham Palace, the Eiffel Tower! The Arc de Triomphe. But for now, all we have is an attic above Amsterdam, so I must go back to the others. Be good and you'll be happy tomorrow.

Anne I'm happy tonight. Very happy. I might be in love.

Otto I know. We're not blind. But boys can spell trouble.

Anne Peter's different.

Otto Anne! Please stop dreaming.

Anne I'll try. Daddy! What will become of us?

Otto *smiles and floats away.*

Scene Five

The other people fade. Jazz music plays.

Anne Come on, Peter. Are you coming or not?

Peter Ay, ay, Captain.

Anne We've raised anchor. Jump aboard.

Peter Where we sailing?

Anne To the future.

Peter In that case don't go without me.

Anne All aboard the *Rotterdam*. The huge ocean liner. We are all at sea.

Peter And the moon on the water and you in my arms. Shall we canoodle?

Anne Land ahoy! We're there!

Peter Where?

Anne Hollywood, of course.

The cast become smiling dwarfs. Except for **Mrs Van Daan** *who is the Wicked Queen.*

All   The bear went over the mountain,
       The bear went over the mountain,
       The bear went over the mountain,
       To see what he could see.

       And all that he could see,
       And all that he could see,
       Was the other side of the mountain,
       The other side of the mountain,
       The other side of the mountain
       Was all that he could see.

Anne Snow White was the most beautiful princess, but somehow she wasn't real, not flesh and blood.

Mrs Van Daan Mirror! Mirror! on the wall, who is the prettiest, nastiest of them all? You are! Come over here!

Anne Careful! The Wicked Queen!

Peter *automatically goes towards his mother.*

Where are you going?

Peter Don't worry. I'll settle her.

Anne Goodbye, Peter.

Peter Mother! I must tell you something.

Mrs Van Daan Sit down.

Peter *obeys and* **Mrs Van Daan** *sits on him.*

Peter Mother! I'm in love . . .

Anne *sings 'I'm Wishing' by Frank Churchill.*

Anne (*singing*)	I'm wishing –
Margot (*her echo*)	I'm wishing –
Anne	For the one I love, to find me
Margot	To find me
Anne	Today.
Margot	Today.
Anne	I'm hoping
Margot	I'm hoping
Peter	And I'm dreaming of, the nice things
Margot	The nice things
Anne	He'll say
Margot	He'll say.

Peter I'm in love with Anne.

Margot I can see that Peter is just perfect for you, Anne. You have my blessing.

Anne Thank you. This is a dream and a half.

Otto Right! Let's wrap this up.

Edith All we want is a happy ending.

Anne Ladies and gentlemen. I have an important announcement to make. Peter and I are getting married.

Anne *and* **Margot** *embrace.*

Peter Are we?

Anne Yes.

Peter When?

Anne Now. Right now.

Peter Are we?

Anne I love you.

Margot He'll make a beautiful brother-in-law.

Anne (*to* **Margot**) I'm so happy.

The sisters embrace and the scene darkens as the people make improvised musical wedding sounds. **Anne** *takes a sheet from her bed and wraps it around her, improvising a wedding gown. The* *women get another sheet and the four parents raise it above their heads, each holding a corner. This becomes a wedding canopy.*

Stars! Trees! The full moon by my crown. Look!

The dark becomes a mass of stars. The bells sound happily.

The whole universe witness to our wedding. And even God is somewhere quite close. Can't you smell him?

They all sniff.

Edith Just smoke. I can just smell smoke.

Peter *and* **Anne** *stand together under the canopy.* **Dussel** *becomes a cantor, sings a wedding prayer, holds up a wine glass and places it under* **Peter***'s foot.*

Dussel To remind us of the destruction of the Temple.

Anne We've got long memories. Smash it, Peter.

Peter *does so.*

All *Mazeltov.* Good luck.

Otto *and* **Mr Van Daan** *embrace and start a slow Eastern European dance.*

Men '*Chosan chola mazeltov* – dada – deedee – dadada' –

The others join in but **Anne** *commands them to freeze as she and* **Peter** *dance slowly together.*

Anne What about the wedding feast?

Peter You are the wedding feast.

Everyone else is seated for a meal. But the wedding is over. We are back to our reality of the attic.

Edith Come and get it! Tulip bulb and potato soup!

Peter Dreams are over. Back to who we are. Back to where we are.

Scene Six

Anne Amsterdam. August the fourth, nineteen forty-four.

Air-raid outside.

Edith The war is nearly over and we shall be free.

Anne Free!

Edith What?

Anne Nothing. (*She smiles, trying to hide her foreboding.*)

Edith Tell me the truth. What do you see?

Anne I see peace. Perfect and beautiful peace. And I love you both, forever. (*She hugs her mother and father.*)

Edith
Mrs Van Daan } (*together*) Soup! Soup! Who wants soup? Lunchtime. Come and get it.

The others eat.

Mrs Van Daan Join in, Anne! That's your trouble. You never join in.

Peter This soup is wonderful. Ugh!

Edith Lunch will do for supper tomorrow, so let's all have breakfast tonight.

Margot After this war and the end of this nightmare I want to go out into the streets of Amsterdam and kiss the very first handsome young man I meet and fall in love and get married and have five children.

Mrs Van Daan You'll be lucky.

Margot I've not given up hope. Where there's life there's hope. And I know that all this will soon be a thing of the past and we'll get on and live our lives to the full.

Peter Eat! That's my philosophy. Eat while you can. Live for the moment.

Anne Boys! All they think about. Their stomachs.

Peter *is lost in eating.* **Anne** *goes to leave.*

Edith Where are you going, darling?

Anne I need fresh air. I need to escape. I need to see my beautiful city. Just once more. I need to stretch and breathe the sky.

Edith (*humouring her*) Yes, darling. Don't we all.

Anne *tries the trapdoor.*

Darling. What are you doing?

Anne The empty ballroom of dreams. (*She sings.*)
Dancing in the dark till the tune ends,
We're dancing in the dark – and it soon ends –
We're waltzing in the wonder of why we're here –
Time hurries by – we're here and gone . . .

Anne *floats into an empty square. Amsterdam at night. There are searchlights and the crump of bombs.*

Come, bombs! Come, fire! Devour the Nazi monster. Even destroy my beloved Amsterdam if you have to.

Outside Inside

Outside inside
Two worlds apart
Inside we argue
Outside we part
Inside we're safe
But we fight for a chair
Outside we're taken
To God knows where
Outside inside
Two worlds apart
Inside we argue
Outside the broken heart
And sky and travel and death

Outside the Royal Palace. A man (**Dussel**) *stalks her.*

Man What are you doing in the streets, child? In the middle of the night?

Anne Looking for my childhood.

Man But surely you want to grow up?

Anne Yes. But I'm afraid. I want life to go backwards.

Man Ah yes, I thought you were in pain. Can I tell you about my hobby? I am totally obsessed with military bands. I would follow any band, good or bad, to the ends of the earth and often do in my imagination. As soon as I get home I immediately start the military music on my radiogram. I know every march ever written, almost every band that ever played, their particular style. There in my living-room I march, back and forth, back and forth, every lunch-time, every night. It is a wonderful exercise and I can assure you it is a morally uplifting and spiritual experience. The Germans are a humane race, compassionate. I know you are afraid because of the things you have heard they have done or are about to do. A lot of this you can disregard. It is propaganda. I maintain that soon you will notice a big change. An occupying power is bound to take actions that seem draconian and excessively harsh early on. The Jews are merely an expediency, a scapegoat for our ambitions. It is almost understandable, even if a little painful. Open up. (*He has become Hitler and wants to probe into* **Anne***'s mouth.*) Where's my scalpel?

Anne Here!

She takes the knife from his white coat pocket, thrusts it into his stomach.

Man Help me! Help me! *Heil –*

He raises his arm, calling to her, but his cry becomes Hitler's fanatical call to his followers.

Heil! Heil!

Massed crowds shout 'Heil!' in reply.

Anne Hitler's dead. (*She is by the radio.*)

Edith (*coming to* **Anne**) What are you doing up, this time of night?

Anne Mother! (*She whispers in* **Edith***'s ear.*)

Edith What?

Anne It's true! It's true!

Edith What are you saying?

Anne *again whispers in her ear.*

How do you know?

Anne It must be true. It must be so. They announced it on the radio.

Edith It's wonderful! Wake up, everyone! It's wonderful!

Mrs Van Daan (*emerging from sleep*) What's happening?

Edith It's true. (*She whispers into* **Mrs Van Daan***'s ear.*)

Mrs Van Daan Are you sure?

Edith It's true!

Mrs Van Daan How do you know?

Edith Anne heard it on the radio. It's official!

Mrs Van Daan *kisses* **Edith** *and dances with her.*

Mrs Van Daan Wake up, everyone! Wake up. It's true. It's official.

One by one, the rest emerge from sleep, yawning and still barely comprehending.

All What is it? Is it the end of the world?

Mrs Van Daan It's wonderful. It's unbelievable. It's official.

Dussel Wait! How do we know it's true?

All Yes! How do we know? How do we know?

Edith It must be true. It must be so. She heard it on the radio.

Anne It must be true. It must be so. I heard it on the radio.

All now move ritualistically, building up to a climax, the song spurring them on. They all sing.

    Hitler Is Dead

All   Hitler is dead!
        Hitler is dead!
        Shot in the head.
        Butchered in bed.

Maggots are crawling
Inside his head.
His eyeballs are jelly,
He's skewered through the belly.
He's mangled and minced
And we are convinced
That Hitler is dead.
Hitler is dead. Hitler is dead.
Strangled in bed.
Strangled in bed.
They've sawn off his thighs,
Sucked out his eyes.
Slugs in his sockets,
Rats in his pockets.
Battered and shattered,
Shattered and battered.
They've scattered his head,
His fingers, his toes,
His heart, his nose.
His fingers, his toes,
His heart, his nose.
Hitler is dead! Dead!
Dead! Dead!
Dead dead dead. *Dead*!

When the song ends they are drained, shattered.

Scene Seven

Mr Van Daan Let's celebrate! I've been saving something special.

They laugh as **Mr Van Daan** *brings out a bottle of wine from his secret hiding-place.*

Dussel Are we sure? Who heard this news?

Anne I did. On the radio.

Mr Van Daan (*looking down through the trapdoor*) Nothing's different in the street.

Dussel (*twiddling the radio*) Everything's the same. Nothing's new. It's not true.

Edith Anne, is it true?

Otto Is it true? Is it true?

Anne It must be true. He must be dead. I want him to be dead. Dad! Mummy! Please let him be dead.

Edith *whispers to her husband.*

Mrs Van Daan Liar! Liar! How could you do this to us? (*Suddenly she attacks* **Anne***, pulling her hair.*)

Mr Van Daan (*trying to restrain his wife*) Angel face! Please!

Edith She's only a child. She's only a child! It was a joke. You understand jokes.

Mr Van Daan It was a bad joke, Anne. The time for jokes is over.

Anne *is crying.*

Edith (*stroking* **Anne***'s hair*) Take no notice, darling. She means well but she's stupid . . .

Mrs Van Daan Me? Stupid? Did you call me stupid?

Otto Silence! Or we'll be discovered.

They all start whispering.

Mrs Van Daan This is the worst thing that ever happened to me. This dreaming, thinking and writing. It leads to trouble. It should be stopped. That girl should face reality.

Otto Anne, she's right. You must stop dreaming.

Anne Without dreams, what are we?

Edith Anne! I understand. But we all have to grow up.

Anne Look what the grown ups have done to this world. Hitler must be dead. He must be dead.

Mrs Van Daan (*angrily*) Peter! Stay away from her.

Peter Yes, Mother.

Otto Stay away from him.

Anne Yes, Father.

Mr Van Daan We mean it, young man! And go to bed.

All disperse, fading into the shadows as the lights concentrate on **Anne** *and* **Peter**.

Peter Yes, Father. I love you, Anne. Forever.

Anne I love you until the end of the world.

Peter And this is true and not a dream.

Anne But dreams are also true. The truth of your deep, inner self.

Peter You're writing all this down, aren't you?

Anne Yes.

Peter Read your diary to me. Please. All of it. Now.

Anne No one else must ever read my diary. My secrets. My truth.

Peter Am I in your diary?

Anne What do you think?

Peter Please show me your diary.

Anne Now?

Peter Now. Please.

Anne I must tell you this. I love you with this kiss.

They kiss.

At least we have this.

Peter At least we have this. I love you with this kiss.

They kiss again.

Anne I would have loved a lifetime of this.

Anne *opens her diary. A terrible wind blows. All the doors fly open. The diary flies out of her hand.*

No. Not yet? I haven't finished yet. (*She sings.*)

Helping Hand!
Please help me.
Turn back the clock.
Save us in time.

Peter What's happening?

Anne We are betrayed.

Peter How? Who?

The door comes off its hinges. Smoke pours in. German voices are heard.

Anne Does it matter now? We're going on a journey.

Suddenly we hear people rushing upstairs, shouting, spiralling, echoing voices.

Voices Raus! Raus! Juden raus! Schnell! Schnell!

Menacing sounds drown everything. Then silence and blinding light.

Anne Just as my world opens, it closes. Just as I stop being a child I stop being. In my beginning is my end.

Train sounds.

Night and fog. Night and fog.

Fog envelops them and in the darkness a thin light shines on all our people. They have become a mass, a sort of box-car. We concentrate on each face in turn.

Mrs Van Daan Why?

Mr Van Daan Why?

Margot Why?

Edith Why?

Otto Why?

Peter Why?

Dussel Why?

Scene Eight

The sound of trains wailing, chugging. The cast all wear yellow stars.

Anne Dreams are over. The nightmare starts. Night and fog. Night and fog. Night and fog. (*Throughout this train scene she continues to repeat this litany.*)

Dussel Why are humans doing this to humans? Why?

Mrs Van Daan Goodbye! Goodbye. Goodbye, Amsterdam.

Mr Van Daan Goodbye, world. Family. Friends.

Margot We didn't ask much from life. We just wanted to live it.

Edith Remember us. Bear witness.

Otto This is the end of the end of the end.

Margot Who will remember us? Who will know we were here?

They undress to reveal identical prison-camp clothing.

All '*A-NI MA-MIN. A-NI MA-MIN. AN-I MA-MIN. Be-e-emu-no shiel mo be-vi-as, Ha-mo-shi-ach-be-vi-as ha-mo-shi-ach a-ni ma min-ve af al pi she yis ma-me-ach im kol zeh a-ni ma-min.*'

They exit one at a time through the back door.

Anne *remains alone.*

Anne (*chanting, translating the gist of their final prayer*) 'I believe that the Messiah will come. And even though he is a little late I will still believe.' People of the World. Save us. Before it's too late. I'm trying to hear your voice, your protest. Children of the world, remember me. I was born. I lived for a while. I fell in love and then I went back into the dark. (*She dances.*) Life is the beautiful light in the entire darkness of time. I dance. Dance because I believe that I exist and I love and I will exist and love forever. Against all the odds. We are beautiful, and yes, we are loving. And we will love one another. One day. All of us. Everywhere. You'll see. Before I go down into the dark, into the night and fog, please remember me. And peace will come. And a thousand centuries of leaves and wind and rain and snow will cover the snow, again and again. And people will come and go. And fall in love. And peace will come. And peace will come. Goodbye, Diary.

Anne *kisses her diary and reluctantly discards it, putting it down upon the pile of clothes heaped on the stage, and she exits through the back door, following the others.*

Her diary seems to light up the darkness that now envelops everything.

Scene Nine

Otto *enters.*

Otto We were in that attic for two years. Until we were betrayed. And then we were taken on that terrible journey, to Auschwitz, where millions of us died, by gas. The war was almost over. Margot and Anne were moved to Germany. It was March, nineteen forty-five. Anne was fifteen. There, in Bergen-Belsen, Margot and Anne died from typhus. Desolate. Alone. A few weeks later the German army surrendered. It was that close. Irony. Anyway, it was all over. All our children went up together, into that exodus, into the clouds, leaving us behind, with dreams, memories, fragments of time. But sometimes I can hear their laughter upon the wind. Her book is special, yet what can replace the laughter of a living child? Anne's book is a marvel, because it contains and captures the hopes and the dreams and the fears of a girl who bore witness to the fact that we were here. That we were cut off and denied our lives, so cruelly. But words are inadequate. This book is precious, yet it is only a book and life is the most precious thing of all. All the books ever written cannot be weighed against the value of one child's life. I would gladly swap it, throw it away, or have it unwritten if I could only have Anne again, living. (*He closes the diary.*)

Blackout.

Curtain.

Furniture and Property List

Act I

On stage: Triangular pile of clothes. *On it*: **Anne**'s diary
              Table
              Upturned chair
              1930s radiogram

Off stage: Yellow star (for **Anne**)
              Tablecloth
              Lighted clothes
              Sheets
              Satchel containing exercise books, pens, scent
                  bottle, copy of *Emil and the Detectives*, photographs,
                  pencils, comb, letters, elastic bands
              Hairbrush
              Boxes, cases, blankets (**Frank** family)
              Various belongings, including an iron and playing
              cards (**Van Daans**)
              Birthday cake
              Various belongings (**Dussel**)

Personal: **Dussel**: business card, knife in pocket

Act II

Off stage: Potty
              Gingerbread house
              Doll
               Wine glass
               Bottle of wine
              Yellow stars (for cast)

Lighting Plot

Act I

To open: Blackout

Cue 1	**Otto** enters *Bring up spot on* **Otto**	(Page 37)
Cue 2	**Otto** opens the diary *Crossfade to spot on* **Anne**	(Page 38)
Cue 3	**Anne**: '. . . evening star, yellow star' *Crossfade to full general lighting*	(Page 38)
Cue 4	**Anne**: 'Going into hiding' *Dim lighting*	(Page 40)
Cue 5	To open Scene 4 *Crossfade to general lighting with daylight through window*	(Page 44)
Cue 6	**Anne**: 'What are you waiting for?' *Change lighting*	(Page 44)
Cue 7	**Anne**: 'Someone walked over my grave' *Revert to previous lighting*	(Page 45)
Cue 8	**Anne** goes to the window *Fade daylight effect to dark through window, dim lighting overall*	(Page 49)
Cue 9	The all-clear sounds *Increase to daylight effect, decrease to night time effect; increase to daylight*	(Page 51)
Cue 10	**Anne**: 'I wish this day was over' *Gradually fade to dark*	(Page 59)
Cue 11	**Anne**: '. . . finest snow you ever saw' *Snow effect*	(Page 62)

Act II

To open: General lighting

Cue 12	**Anne**: 'Hop aboard my dream' *Change to dream sequence lighting*	(Page 67)
Cue 13	To open Scene 4 *Night effect*	(Page 71)
Cue 14	To open Scene 5 *Moonlight effect*	(Page 73)
Cue 15	**Anne**: 'Hollywood, of course' *Dream sequence lighting*	(Page 74)
Cue 16	The sisters embrace *Dim lighting*	(Page 75)
Cue 17	**Anne**: 'Look!' *Starlight effect*	(Page 76)
Cue 18	Everyone else is seated for a meal *Bring up general lighting*	(Page 76)
Cue 19	**Anne** floats into an empty square *Change to exterior night effect with searchlights*	(Page 78)
Cue 20	**Anne**: 'Hitler's dead' *Crossfade to interior darkness*	(Page 79)
Cue 21	**Anne**: 'I heard it on the radio' *Increase lighting*	(Page 80)
Cue 22	**Mr Van Daan**: 'And go to bed' *Dim overall lighting; concentrate on* **Anne** *and* **Peter**	(Page 83)
Cue 23	Menacing sounds drown everything *Intense, bright light*	(Page 84)
Cue 24	**Anne**: 'In my beginning is my end' *Cut to darkness; then bring up light on cast*	(Page 84)
Cue 25	**Anne** remains alone *Spot on* **Anne**	(Page 85)

Cue 26	**Anne** exits	(Page 86)
	Reduce spot to diary	
Cue 27	**Otto** closes the diary	(Page 86)
	Blackout	

Effects Plot

Please read the notices on page iv regarding the use of copyright music and recordings.

Act I

Cue 1	**Anne**: 'Goodbye, House' *House (Edith's taped voice) as script page 41*	(Page 41)
Cue 2	**Anne** takes her diary and opens it *Diary voice as script page 42*	(Page 42)
Cue 3	**Anne** twiddles the radio dial *Victory 'V' drumbeat; Announcer's voice as script page 45, then dance band music plays softly*	(Page 45)
Cue 4	They laugh *Cut music*	(Page 45)
Cue 5	**Margot**: 'A bit, maybe' *Sirens*	(Page 51)
Cue 6	**Anne**: 'The tracery is so beautiful' *Sounds of bombs falling; continue, gradually growing nearer*	(Page 51)
Cue 7	**Otto** returns to the game *All-clear siren sounds*	(Page 51)
Cue 8	**Anne** twiddles the radio knob *Radio interference; voices of Churchill and Announcer with air-raid siren and bombing as script pages 57–9*	(Page 57)
Cue 9	**Edith**: 'There's still a long way to go' *Vera Lynn sings 'Silver Wings in the Moonlight' on radio*	(Page 60)
Cue 10	**Dussel** (*singing*): '. . . Slash away cloud' *Sudden noise outside and crash*	(Page 63)

Act II

Cue 11	**Peter**: '. . . you run right into' *Anti-aircraft shells and bomb sounds reverberate*	(Page 71)
Cue 12	To open Scene 5 *Jazz music*	(Page 73)
Cue 13	**Anne**: 'Look!' *Bells sound happily*	(Page 76)
Cue 14	**Anne**: '. . . nineteen forty-four' *Sounds of an air-raid*	(Page 77)
Cue 15	**Anne**: '. . . we're here and gone . . .' *Crump of bombs*	(Page 78)
Cue 16	**Man**: '*Heil! Heil!*' *Mass crowds shouting* 'Heil!'	(Page 79)
Cue 17	**Anne** opens her diary *Terrible wind blows*	(Page 83)
Cue 18	**Peter**: 'How? Who?' *Smoke; German voices as script page 84, menacing sounds*	(Page 84)
Cue 19	**Anne**: 'In my beginning is my end' *Train sounds; continue in Scene 8 and increase in volume*	(Page 84)
Cue 20	**Anne**: 'Night and fog' *Dry ice*	(Page 85)

Exploring Some of the Issues

Prejudice is an opinion formed beforehand, often an unfavourable one based on inadequate facts. It may be based on a belief or it may be caused by the way someone acts, their appearance or race.

It often causes suffering and can lead to hatred and intolerance. It can lead to violence, the destruction of property and murder. It can often be brought on by fear of the unknown, fear of a perceived or actual difference, or feelings of inadequacy.

When the victims of prejudice are just 'other' people, and not friends or relatives, then very often it does not bother us and we might even make jokes about the situation or at least join in the laughter – so as not to be excluded.

If one becomes the victim of prejudice, and we have the support of family, friends or people like ourselves we can be strong enough to cope with insults, rejection and even hostility. It's more difficult when those from whom you would normally expect support withdraw it, and you become isolated.

Whatever our own prejudices, there will always be people who have other prejudices, and their prejudices could include us. It is very dangerous when prejudice becomes widespread, because then it appears that people have 'permission' to behave in a hostile way and this becomes seen as 'acceptable'. This is what happened under the Nazis in Germany in the 1930s.

Discrimination is unfair treatment of a person, a racial group, or any minority. Prejudice which leads to the different treatment of a certain group of people is called discrimination. It soon gets out of hand – people can be refused service in shops, housing, work, medical treatment or even refused entry to a country.

Propaganda is the organized dissemination of information and allegations to assist or damage the cause of a country, a government or a movement.

Discussion points
1. What is the origin of the word prejudice?
2. How do we learn prejudice? Where does it come from?
3. Are there groups in this country who are victims of prejudice? Who are they and what effect does prejudice have in their lives?
4. Have you ever been a victim of prejudice, or seen an incident in which someone was behaving in a prejudiced way?
5. Is propaganda effective? Why?
   Is it ever justified? Can you give examples?
6. Is there a link between propaganda and advertising?

Dreams of Anne Frank and history

Explain the relative importance of several linked causes, e.g. The causes of the Second World War.

Show an understanding of how causes, motives and consequences may be related, e.g. present . . . the causes of WWII, making connections . . .

Demonstrate how historical interpretations depend on the selection of sources, e.g. compare Anne's accounts of the restrictive legislation directed against the Jews with other sources.

Show how attitudes and circumstances can influence an individual's interpretation of history, e.g. try to find records showing the different reactions to the invasion of Poland and the invasion of Holland and Britain's decision to declare war.

Make deductions from historical sources. Look for accounts written by other people who hid like Anne did; also look for accounts of the Kindertransport children who were brought to Britain before the war started. Describe what living in Holland was like after the German invasion for Jews and non-Jews. Compare the experiences of those children who were sent away to the ones who remained.

Comment on the usefulness of an historical source by reference to its content, as evidence of a particular enquiry, e.g. how successful were the Germans in persuading the Dutch to obey their new laws?

Make judgements about the reliability and value of historical sources by reference to the circumstances in which they were produced, e.g. how effective is Anne's diary as a description of the effect on Dutch life of the German invasion of the Netherlands?

The experience of war. What was the experience and impact of war in Europe? What effect did the Holocaust have on the lives of Europeans?

Learning from the past

First they arrested the Communists – but I was not a Communist, so I did nothing. Then they came for the Social Democrats – but I was not a Social Democrat, so I did nothing. Then they arrested the trade unionists – but I did nothing because I was not one. And then they came for the Jews and then the Catholics, but I was neither a Jew nor a Catholic and I did nothing. At last they came and arrested me – and there was no one left to do anything about it.

Rev. Martin Niemoller, a German Protestant clergyman
first printed in *The Times*, London, 11th October, 1937

History: World War II
1. What was happening in Germany when Anne Frank's family left and moved to the Netherlands? (1933)
2. What was happening in the war when Anne and her family went into hiding? (July 1942)
3. What happened when they were captured and how soon after she died did the war end?
4. How important was Amsterdam and the Netherlands to both the Germans and the Allies in the war?

English

Themes for discussion, reading and writing – use poetry, prose, diary entries, newspaper accounts or eyewitness radio reports: prejudice, imprisonment, heroism, loyalty, families, bullying, friendship, betrayal, dreams, nightmares, first love, isolation, where we live, trusting people, working together, caring for other people.

Arts and technology

Some project suggestions:

1. Find examples of the use of art in propaganda.
2. Compare the art of the Third Reich with that of the Weimar Republic.

Religious education

Some possible projects:

1. Find out what you can about Judaism.
2. Compare the customs, stories and games of other religions.

Had Anne Frank, a typical child, lived next door, could she have counted on us for help during the Nazi regime?

Would we have recognized the dangers of fascism, or would we have believed the propaganda that depicted Jews as inferior, untrustworthy citizens? Would we have agreed with those who singled out the Jews as the cause of all evil – just as some people today feel free to blame 'the foreigners' for all their ills? Or would we have continued – perhaps with a feeling of powerlessness – our daily routine?

Many Germans did, in fact, continue their daily routine. They were not alone. The Dutch and other people, as well, acted in the same way without even being aware of their action, or – as it turns out – their lack of action. This indifference, this resignation, this fear, this selfishness – all of these are widespread human characteristics. Therefore, the chances are today, too, people all over the world are left to meet their fate, just like the Frank family.

Even the help of some individuals could not prevent the deportation and extermination of Anne Frank and millions of others.

The rejection and prevention of discrimination must start at an early stage and each of us has a personal responsibility toward achieving this goal. Had these convictions shaped the human consciousness in the 1930s, then the name Hitler would be totally insignificant to us today.

Anti-Semitism and Anti-Zionism

Recently, violent anti-Semitic actions have spread fear among the Jewish community in Western Europe. For many, it is an unbearable idea that fifty years after the end of World War II Jewish organizations are forced to use safety measures and ask for police support.

Apart from hard, violent anti-Semitism that reminds us of the hate against Jews during World War II, anti-Semitism sometimes takes the form of anti-Zionism. It is not always clear at what point anti-Zionism becomes anti-Semitism. Anti-Zionism rejects the state of Israel as a Jewish state, which is not the same as criticizing certain policies of the Israeli Government.

Often however, one can surmise that criticism of the Israeli Government is, in fact, based on the denial of the right of the state of Israel to exist as a Jewish state. Compared to other states, isn't Israel judged by different standards, and if so, how has that come about? When the Israeli Government takes action, not only the Government is judged but all Jews everywhere are held responsible. In this way criticism of the state of Israel is used as justification for anti-Semitism.

Anne Frank and the Future

The play is not just about the past. It is also about now and about the future. It is about Nazi Germany; about Bosnia; about Albania, China; Chechnia. It is about us.

The story and the spirit of Anne Frank stands in a no man's land; a doorway that reflects both past and present. The past leads straight to the future. We stand in that doorway, knowing it is up to us; we cannot turn a blind eye to racism and discrimination. We are the witnesses who must stand up against aquiescence.

The diary reveals the almost impossible events of the past, but we now know that those events were not the end of something. Nazism was the beginning of something. Of a new dark age. The Nazis were the prophets of this new dark age and their philosophy must not go unchallenged. Petty nationalism and racism must be confronted whenever they raise their terrible hydra heads. If we think we are better than others, we are committing that crime of taking away the humanity of others; dehumanizing other human beings.

Intolerance and hatred still breeds amongst us; these are the greatest threats to life upon this earth, threats that will engulf the entire human family unless we confront the siren voices of nationalism that scream the lie that we are better than our neighbours.

Anne's diary is both a symbol and a warning. Its stark message is now more apposite than ever. Anne's diary is about the spirit of creativity that thrives, despite the hatred and the horror that humans have brought upon this world and themselves. The lessons of the Holocaust have not been learned. The terrible truth is that Anne died alone, in abject misery, all hope gone from her young life. She so loved and wanted to love; but in the end she was the victim of the dark forces, the anti-life. W. H. Auden wrote, 'We must love one another or die.'

Coda

Anne's story defies logic. Unlike the other persons hiding in the attic, Anne did not take refuge in boredom or melancholy or anger; neither did she retreat into herself. Instead she made use of her incarceration by allowing her mind the freedom of soaring beyond the captivity of her tiny world. Thus she turned despair into creative energy and she eternally remains, a lone and shimmering icon against the darkness and madness of our times.

Anne Frank did not give in to despair; she disregarded her perilous surrounding, made inward journeys to expand her horizons. Her life and work seem to have an increasing impact and relevance. Her very specific voice becomes more and more universal. She holds a beacon, becomes a guardian for the human spirit. Her short life lights the way for us all. Somehow she almost balances the horror of the modern world; somehow she guides and inspires us and, against all the odds, makes us believe that there can be a better world.